MICHAEL YOUNG

THE RISE OF THE MERITOCRACY
1870 – 2033

*An Essay on
Education and
Equality*

PENGUIN BOOKS

Penguin Books Ltd, Harmondsworth, Middlesex
AUSTRALIA : Penguin Books Pty Ltd, 762 Whitehorse Road,
Mitcham, Victoria

—

First published by Thames and Hudson 1958
Published in Penguin Books 1961

—

Copyright © Thames and Hudson, 1958

—

Made and printed in Great Britain
by Western Printing Services Ltd,
Bristol

PELICAN BOOKS

A 485

THE RISE OF THE MERITOCRACY
1870–2033

MICHAEL YOUNG

CONTENTS

CONTENTS

PART TWO: DECLINE OF THE LOWER CLASSES

'The courage and imagination with which the development plan is drawn, the energy and judgement with which it is carried into effect, will not only determine the future of our educational system, but may largely shape the future course of the nation's forward march.'

The Nation's Schools
Ministry of Education, 1945

ACKNOWLEDGEMENTS

The author would like to acknowledge the valuable help and encouragement received from: A. L. Bacharach, Vincent Brome, Daphne Chandler, Margaret Cole, C. A. R. Crosland, Dorothy Elmhirst, Jean Floud, Geoffrey Gorer, A. H. Halsey, Irving Kristol, Peter Marris, Enid Mills, Edward Shils, J. H. Smith, Prudence Smith, R. H. Tawney, Peter Townsend, Peter Willmott, Leonard Woolf, Joan Young.

INTRODUCTION

WHAT was the connexion between the gutting of the Ministry of Education and the attempt on the life of the Chairman of the T.U.C.? Between the unofficial transport strike and the equally unofficial walk-out of domestic servants? All these questions are rendered doubly topical by the general strike which the Populists have called for the coming May, on the first anniversary of the troubles. Will there be a response? Will 2034 repeat 1789 or merely 1848? I would submit that more topical, and more important, a subject could hardly be discussed. It touches on a clear and present danger to the state.

The Prime Minister, in his frank report to the House of Lords, put part of the responsibility for the May Affair upon administrative failings. The wrecking of Wren's store at Stevenage the Prime Minister regards as a local disturbance; its 2,000 shop assistants were undoubtedly incensed by the management's unexpected rejection of the four-day week. Destruction of the atomic station at South Shields might never have happened with a less provocative director. The walk-out of domestic servants was precipitated by the slowness of the Price Review, similar trouble in the other Provinces of Europe being evidence enough for that. Feeling against the Education Ministry was stimulated by the publication in April of the last report of the Standing Commission on the National Intelligence, and so on. All this I readily accept, yet it is not the whole story. We also have to explain why administrative miscalculations, that in an ordinary year would have passed almost unnoticed, should on this occasion have provoked such fierce and concerted protest. To understand what happened, and so be prepared for what is going to happen, we have to take the measure of the Populist movement, with its strange blend of women in the lead and men in the rank and file.

The women's circles have produced evangelists before; their eclipse has usually been as sudden as their rising. Not so the leaders by whom we are now plagued. They have consolidated their strength. The Convention they organized at Leicester shortly before Christmas 2032 was their decisive moment. The women's circles would be mustered – that was well known; the women's sections of the Technicians' Party would be there – that was half allowed for. What was not expected was the attendance of so many representatives, men as well as women, from local branches of the Party and the Unions. In defiance of their leaders, they came from all over the country, and particularly from the North of England and Scotland – this hostility to London and the South is a sinister aspect of the agitation too much played down by government sociologists. Even the Association of Scientific Benefactors was represented. From Leicester sprang the ill-assorted conglomeration which has come to be known as the Populist Movement, with its strange charter. For the only time within living memory a dissident minority from the élite has struck up an alliance with the lower orders, hitherto so isolated and so docile. Their union fomented the local incidents in Kirkcaldy and Stevenage, South Shields and White-hall, into the national crisis of last May.

What does it all mean? Only the historians of the future will know, perhaps even they will not agree. Close as we are to the crisis, with every day bringing fresh news, it is impossible for anyone to be more than tentative in his opinions. No consensus has yet formed. The official view is that such an alliance across class-lines is a misalliance, the background of leaders and led so different, and the common interest between them so slight, that the movement cannot last. The *Sunday Scientist* has in a much-quoted, if scurrilous, phrase likened some of the leaders to 'Rimsky-Korsakov in a Lyons Corner House'. Has Somerville vulgarized itself without finding any deep response? I think not, at least I do not agree about the response. The Populists could not have gathered such momentum, the May Affair reached such dimensions, unless there were more than passing resentments to feed on. My reading is that these resentments have their roots deep in history.

*

The purpose of this essay is to discuss some of the historical causes of the grievances that erupted in the May risings. My theme is that, whether or not these were explicitly organized by the Populists, they were certainly organized by history. One belief is implicit throughout: there are no revolutions, only the slow accretions of a ceaseless change that reproduces the past while transforming it. I am not thinking of the thousand and one technical innovations which have, from one point of view, made of the last century an aeon. These commonplaces I will not deal with but rather try to show that, however odd our great-grandfathers may now seem, the twenty-first century is woven on the same loom as neo-Elizabethan times. I shall illustrate my essay with references to the period, between 1914 and 1963, on which I specialized at the Manchester Grammar School. I would like to acknowledge my debt to my sixth-form master, Mr Woodcock, for first pointing out to me how revealing a study of that time could be for an understanding of the progress man has made in the last century. He first introduced me to historical sociology as it has been developed in the ancient universities.

At the beginning of my special period, 1914, the upper classes had their fair share of geniuses and morons, so did the workers; or, I should say, since a few brilliant and fortunate working men always climbed up to the top despite having been subordinate in society, the inferior classes contained *almost* as high a proportion of superior people as the upper classes themselves. Intelligence was distributed more or less at random. Each social class was, in ability, the miniature of society itself; the part the same as the whole. The fundamental change of the last century, which was fairly begun before 1963, is that intelligence has been redistributed between the classes, and the nature of the classes changed. The talented have been given the opportunity to rise to the level which accords with their capacities, and the lower classes consequently reserved for those who are also lower in ability. The part is no longer the same as the whole.

The rate of social progress depends upon the degree to which power is matched with intelligence. The Britain of a century ago squandered its resources by condemning even talented people to manual work; and blocked the efforts of members of the lower classes to obtain just recognition for their abilities. But Britain could not be a caste society if it was to survive as a great nation, great, that is, in comparison with others. To withstand international competition the country had to make better use of its human material, above all, of the talent which was even in England, one might say always

and everywhere, too scarce. Schools and industries were
progressively thrown open to merit, so that the clever
children of each generation had opportunity for ascent.
The proportion of people with I.Q.s over 130 could not
be raised – the task was rather to prevent a fall – but
the proportion of such people in work which called upon
their full capacities was steadily raised. For every
Rutherford there have in modern times been ten such
magnates, for every Keynes two, and even Elgar has
had a successor. Civilization does not depend upon the
stolid mass, the *homme moyen sensuel*, but upon the crea-
tive minority, the innovator who with one stroke can
save the labour of 10,000, the brilliant few who cannot
look without wonder, the restless élite who have made
mutation a social, as well as a biological, fact. The ranks
of the scientists and technologists, the artists and the
teachers, have been swelled, their education shaped to
their high genetic destiny, their power for good increased. Progress is their triumph; the modern world
their monument.

And yet, if we ignore the casualties of progress, we fall
victim, in the sphere of human relations, to the insidious
complacency which in natural science we so much
deplore. In the balanced view of sociology we have to
consider the failures as well as the successes. Every
selection of one is a rejection of many. Let us be frank
and admit that we have failed to assess the mental state
of the rejected, and so secure their necessary adjustment. The danger that has settled in upon us since the
shock administered by the events of the last year is that
the clamouring throng who find the gates of higher education barred against them may turn against the social
order by which they feel themselves condemned. Do not
the masses, for all their lack of capacity, sometimes

behave as though they suffered from a sense of indignity? Do they necessarily see themselves as we see them? We know it is only by giving free rein to well-trained imagination and organized intelligence that humanity can hope to reach, in centuries to come, the fulfilment it deserves. Let us still recognize that those who complain of present injustice *think* they are talking about something real, and try to understand how it is that nonsense to us makes sense to them.

PART ONE

RISE OF THE ÉLITE

CHAPTER ONE

CLASH OF SOCIAL FORCES

1. CIVIL SERVICE MODEL

THE 1870s have been called the beginning of the modern era not so much because of the Commune as because of Mr Forster. Education was then made compulsory in Britain, patronage at last abolished in the civil service and competitive entry made the rule. Merit became the arbiter, attainment the standard, for entry and advancement in a splendid profession,[1] which was all the more an achievement because so many of our great-grandfathers were positively hostile to 'competition wallahs' in British government. Considering the opposition, it is remarkable that by 1944 the most brilliant young men from Cambridge and Oxford were already going into the administrative class, there to guide the destinies of the nation; outstanding young men from the provincial universities into the hardly less important scientific and technical grades; worthy young men and women from the grammar schools into the executive grades; the less

1. The authors of the Northcote-Trevelyan report were commendably aware of what was needed. 'It would be natural to expect that so important a profession would attract into its ranks the ablest and the most ambitious of the youth of the country; that the keenest emulation would prevail among those who had entered it; and that such as were endowed with superior qualifications would rapidly rise to distinction and public eminence. Such, however, is by no means the case. Admission into the civil service is indeed eagerly sought after, but it is for the unambitious, and the indolent or incapable, that it is chiefly desired.' Northcote-Trevelyan Report on the Organization of the Permanent Civil Service (February 1854).

outstanding joined the junior clerical grades; and the fine body of men and women who were the backbone of the service entered the manual and manipulative grades straight from the elementary (later called secondary modern) schools. Here was a model for any sensible organizer to emulate. It was copied a thousand times in commerce and industry, at first mainly by the large companies like Imperial Chemicals and Unilever, and later by the ever-proliferating public corporations.

The flaw in these otherwise admirable arrangements was, of course, that the rest of society, and in particular education, was not yet run on the civil-service principle. Education was very far from proportioned to merit. Some children of an ability which should have qualified them as assistant secretaries were forced to leave school at fifteen and become postmen. Assistant secretaries delivering letters! – it is almost incredible. Other children with poor ability but rich connexions, pressed through Eton and Balliol, eventually found themselves in mature years as high officers in the Foreign Service. Postmen delivering *démarches*! – what a tragic farce! The civil service, wrestling with an intractable problem, did something to make up for injustice in the larger society by enlarging opportunities for elevation within its own ranks. Particularly in wartime, it substituted late developers from the lower grades for early deterioraters who managed to pass their final examinations only to sink exhausted into the Treasury. Clever clerks could even in peacetime climb on to a quite different ladder; a few of them became executives, and in their later years a few of these broke into the lower ranks of the administrative class. The limits were the deficiencies of the general educational system. Only when the school did its job were the Civil Service Commissioners able to do theirs.

When no more assistant secretaries had to leave school at fifteen, and no more postmen were sent to Balliol, the great reform begun in the 1870s could at last be completed.

The force of this example is difficult to over-estimate. The names in the Imperial Calendar a hundred years ago adorned a civil service renowned, for good reason, as the best in the world. How close the analogy with modern society! Today we have an élite selected according to brains and educated according to deserts, with a grounding in philosophy and administration as well as in the two S's of science and sociology. The administrative class in the old civil service was also picked for brains and given an education which was far more than vocational, and yet had a bearing (like the Roman and unlike that other great Imperial Civil Service, of China) upon the tasks they were later called upon to perform. Today we frankly recognize that democracy can be no more than aspiration, and have rule not so much by the people as by the cleverest people; not an aristocracy of birth, not a plutocracy of wealth, but a true meritocracy[1] of talent. Likewise, the old civil service exercised, with skill and tact, a great deal more power than Parliament because it was so well chosen and well trained. Today each member of the meritocracy has an attested minimum rating of 125 (with the top posts for psychologists, sociologists, and Permanent Secretaries reserved since the Crawley-Jay award of 2018 for the over 160s): has not Tauber's retrospective method

1. The origin of this unpleasant term, like that of 'equality of opportunity', is still obscure. It seems to have been first generally used in the sixties of the last century in small-circulation journals attached to the Labour Party, and gained wide currency much later on.

shown that a century ago the majority of the administrative class already had indices higher than 125? These were the rudiments of the modern system. If today intelligence reigns supreme and in three-quarters of the world unchallenged, a modest tribute must be paid to the far-sighted pioneers of the British civil service. It is an exaggeration, an excusable one, to say that our society is a memorial to them no less than to the early socialists.

2. ALL THINGS BRIGHT AND BEAUTIFUL

Until the civil service reforms the greater part of society was governed by nepotism. In the agricultural world which predominated until well on in the nineteenth century, status was not achievable by merit, but ascribed by birth. Class by class, status by status, occupation by occupation, sons followed faithfully in the footsteps of fathers, and fathers as faithfully behind grandfathers. People did not ask a boy what he was going to be when he grew up; they knew – he was going to work on the land like his ancestors before him. For the most part there was no selection for jobs; there was only inheritance. Rural society (and its religion) was family writ larger.

With the father at the head, the status of the other members of the family was graded in a hierarchy, with eldest son ranking before younger[1] and sons before

1. From the time that primogeniture became generally established, younger sons who had to leave the family threshold were the tillers of achievement and merchants of social change. But until the nineteenth century, population increased but slowly, and it was comparatively rare for there to be more than one son alive to inherit at the death of the father. In my special period the Nazis deliberately reintroduced primogeniture in Germany in order to drive younger sons off the land into the army and to the short-lived colonies in Eastern Europe.

daughters. As in the family so in the village. The lord of the manor was the patriarch, and below him in their proper degrees were the farming population, the freeholders ranking above copyholders, copyholders above cottagers, cottagers above farm servants.

> *The rich man in his castle,*
> *The poor man at his gate,*
> *He made them high and lowly*
> *And ordered their estate.*
> *All things bright and beautiful, etc.*

As in the village, so in the kingdom: the Royal Family, headed by the Father of his country, stood over the orders and estates of the realm. As in the kingdom on earth, so in the Kingdom of Heaven. The same man was always at the head of the table. Such a rule was hardly designed to encourage youthful ambition.

In holding a mirror to the past, even the historian can seldom escape the image of his own inquiring face, and it is practically impossible for any layman, taking for granted as he does the logic of human engineering, to understand the apparent folly of his ancestors. Of course there was tyranny, waste, and rigidity in the old system. But that was not all. Lord Salisbury once said he could not think of a logical defence of the hereditary principle and, for that reason, was disinclined to give it up. He was able to speak with such assurance because, to anyone whose roots were in the countryside,[1] the justification for inheritance when agriculture was a family affair was almost self-evident. Agriculture demanded

1. Things were different in the towns, graced as always, by people of the 'middle sort'; where, in Defoe's words, 'Draymen and Porters fill the City Chair; and Footboys Magisterial Purple wear.'

hard and unremitting exertion, and, in the prevailing mental climate, this was best secured when men knew they were working for children and grandchildren who would benefit from improvement as they would suffer from neglect. Agriculture demanded that the toilers should be attached to the soil, lest the always precarious supply of food should fail, and this attachment was best safeguarded when children were set to learn and love, at an age when they were at their most impressionable, the little peculiarities of the land they would one day inherit. Agriculture demanded that the fertility of the soil should be continuously nourished, not exploited for temporary gain; and the long view was instilled in people who had at heart the interests of posterity, as embodied in their own family. Inheritance at once prompted exertion, instilled responsibility, and preserved continuity.

The soil grows castes; the machine makes classes. The old system was good enough as long as England depended upon primitive agriculture, but as industry grew, feudalism was more and more of a restraint upon efficiency. It was not so much inheritance of property[1] that mattered. Indeed, the more riches a father bequeathed, the more often his children did nothing apart from the labour of spending their money. When the family *was* pensioned off, the power descended from the fathers to paid managers selected for their ability,

1. An amusing instance of the tendency of socialists to live in the past was their continued insistence, long after wealth in land had ceased to count, on the need for equalizing holdings of *property*. Fortunately, as it has turned out, they were very much less concerned with the distribution of power, which is by no means equated with the distribution of wealth in any but an agricultural society. Fenn's first maxim for the student of historical sociology – where goes power, there go I – was not first for nothing.

24

which was just as it should be. What mattered most was the number of children who inherited power and position as well as wealth. It is amazing how many doctors were the sons of doctors, how many lawyers the sons of lawyers – and likewise with professions of many kinds. In industry and commerce, many successful men preferred to send their children up the social ladder into the professions; even in business job succession was quite common enough to be a very serious impediment to productivity. Naturally enough, able fathers did bear able children – though less often before the spread of intelligenic marriages – who were doubly entitled to their power, by merit, as well as birth. But how sadly frequent was the opposite – the son who did not match his father, whose ability was perhaps of a different kind, whose leanings were to art or philosophy instead of business, or whose energy was curdled by the nearness of his parent – and yet down he sat at his father's desk and kept the seat warm for his own son. Many sons did their best, by training and application, to abide by Goethe's instruction:

> Really to own what you inherit
> You first must earn it by your merit.

But what was the use? There are limits to self-deception. Human tragedy was also social waste.[1] Until the Butler

1. The importance of calculating this wastage was urged by one of the most far-sighted pioneers. Professor Hogben said in 1938 that 'we may investigate how far the process of occupational recruitment is based on special aptitude for a particular occupation; and the problem of political arithmetic is then to estimate the remediable wastage due to defective social organization and the loss of social efficiency resulting therefrom'. *Political Arithmetic*, 1938. Some years earlier Kenneth Lindsay had calculated, in an influential book, that proved ability to the extent of at least forty per cent of the nation's children was then being denied expression.

Act began to take effect in the seventies and eighties, Britain was outstanding among industrial countries as the home and fount of nepotism in a hundred subtle forms.

Almost any intelligent observer could see how criminal this was. In the last century countless crises and disasters were caused by the wrong father's son or (sometimes) daughter being in the wrong place at the wrong time. Why then did a system of inheritance suitable to agriculture survive for so long? Britain had been an industrial country for well over a century before it rooted out nepotism. Why such a gap between the end of dependence upon the soil and the end of dependence upon caste? One of the reasons is obvious enough. This island enjoyed a doubtful blessing: it was never invaded, never completely defeated in war, never shaken by political revolution. The country was, in short, never jolted into making a fresh start. As with all countries which decline slowly and steadily, decline, that is, in a stable way, today was never, after 1914, as brilliant as yesterday. Britain lived on ancestral capital, and the more it did so, the more it had to do so; the dimmer the present, the greater the justification for escaping from it. A strange doctrine, I know, for a modern sociologist, but I

Social Progress and Educational Waste, 1924. It was not until much later, however, that Professor Marlow was, on a body of cogent assumptions, able to estimate the wastage in the U.K. as having been equal to about thirty-eight megaunits per annum in the forties, falling to about thirty-three in the sixties, to about eighteen by the nineties and to 5·2 megas in the 2020s. This is said to be the irreducible minimum, or in technical terms the Marlow Line, beyond which social efficiency cannot further be improved. But after all that has happened in the past century, who can safely predict what further progress may still be possible? Nor is the basis of these calculations yet altogether satisfactory.

am not alone in saying that too many people had too sharp a sense of history, along with too dull a sense of what the future might be persuaded to yield. It was not like this in the nineteenth century, but by the middle of the twentieth, tradition was over-valued, continuity too much revered. For every change there had to be precedent. Britain, in other words, remained rural-minded long after eighty per cent of its population were collected together in towns – altogether as strange an example of cultural lag on a mass scale as China before the Mao Dynasty.

Ancestor-worship took the form of reverence for old houses and churches, the most amazing coinage, the quaintest weights and measures. Guards, regiments, public houses, old cars, cricket, above all the hereditary monarchy and in a less obvious way the class around the monarchy, namely the aristocracy, which could trace its descent from a more splendid past. Even politicians, as Privy Councillors, borrowed some of the royal glamour; civil servants coyly called themselves HMG.[1] The State itself had high prestige because it attracted some of the status of the aristocracy who used to govern the government. In the United States (without an aristocracy) it was for long assumed that all government was bad, whereas in Britain people were always indignant that governments were not better. Not only the government, all the most important institutions of the country, from the Universities to the Royal Society, from the Marylebone Cricket Club to the T.U.C., from

1. In England piety never went to quite such an excess as in Japan, where the prevailing sentiment was expressed in a famous poem,

> *Precious are my parents that gave me birth,*
> *So that I might serve His Majesty.*

the merchant marine to Fortnum & Mason, were at one time blessed by royal patronage, and there was hardly a leading company in any industry which could not boast of a peer on its board. The aristocracy was the father-figure in the collective unconscious; its influence so pervasive that brilliant people, successful in their own right, were sometimes ashamed of their lowly origins, instead of proud that they had risen above them. Of all their admired characteristics, the most widely emulated was the habit aristocrats were supposed to have of not working, or rather of exerting themselves only at work which was sanctified by being unpaid.[1] In industry top management slavishly copied these drones. Contemporary accounts show in harrowing detail that as late as 1975 managers of important firms were still behaving (often without knowing why) as though they were 'gentlemen of independent means'. In the army they were not men but officers; in industry not men but gentlemen. They pretended, in a ritualistic way, that they did not have to earn their living at all – managers arrived at their jobs two or three hours after their manual employees; came dressed in a suit cut for the club rather than the factory; occupied an office which looked like a drawing-room, with not a sign to be seen of anything so vulgar as a digital computer; nourished themselves from a cocktail cabinet just like the one at home; ate at the firm's expense in a canteen laid out to look like a private drawing-room; and toiled on late into the evening in the hours for which they were *not* paid. They made work

1. Magazines of the 1960s and 1970s report sightseers enormously impressed by the lords and ladies who acted as guides to the Longleats and Knoles. The glamour of owners who could be admired, and at the same time more pitied than feared, brushed off on their paymasters.

into hobby as much as they made hobby into work: the serious business of life began when they mimicked the sporting squire of old at the first tee.[1] This elaborate pretence was naturally and disastrously imitated by subordinates at every level. Strikes beset the management who tried to stop the labourers from taking time off, at frequent intervals, for tea. The long arm of the aristocracy had productivity securely under arrest.

3. FAMILY AND FEUDALISM

Aristocratic influence would never have lasted so long, even in England, without the support of the family: feudalism and family go together. The family is always the pillar of inheritance. The ordinary parent (not unknown today, we must sorrowfully admit) wanted to hand on his money to his child rather than to outsiders or to the state; the child was part of himself and by bequeathing property to him the father assured a kind of immortality to himself: the hereditary father never died. If parents had a family business which in a sense embodied themselves, they were even more anxious to pass it on to someone of their own blood to manage. Parents, by controlling property, also controlled their children; a threat to cut a child out of a will was almost as effective an assertion of power in industrial as it had

1. The fixation on birds which reached such extraordinary dimensions after the General Election of 1971 was another of the strange legacies of the sporting squire and parson. The old aristocrats bred birds which they tenderly shot, studied their amorous habits with field glasses, and themselves developed the appearance of their quarry. Oscar Wilde said of the English face – 'Once seen, never remembered' – it did not apply to these strange people. Ornithology bridged two worlds by making a pastime for the professional into a science for the amateur.

been in agricultural Britain. Even if they had no property, parents wanted their children to find, if not the same job, then a slightly better job than themselves. Study upon study has shown how impelling these drives were (and are) and how strong the motive possessed by parents to advance their children. To imagine merit where none existed was the sanctioned psychosis of a million homes.

For hundreds of years society has been a battleground between two great principles – the principle of selection by family and the principle of selection by merit. Victory has never gone fully to one principle or the other. The champions of the family have argued that for rearing children there has not yet been any adequate substitute for the device which has served mankind so far. Children raised in orphanages, even the most enlightened, seem to lack the inner assurance needed to convert potential into actual ability. If all went to orphanages, all would have equal opportunity, true, but at the cost of making everyone equally unhappy. Steady affection from the same parents – this has been generally accepted since the experiments in the late 1980s – is necessary for the full glandular development of the infant. Love is biochemistry's chief assistant.

We have had to put up with the failings of the family. We have had to recognize that nearly all parents are going to try to gain unfair advantages for their offspring. The function of society, whose efficiency depends upon observing the principles of selection by merit, is to prevent such selfishness from doing any serious harm. The family is the guardian of individual, the state the guardian of collective efficiency, and this function the State is able to perform because citizens are themselves divided in their interests. As members of a particular family, they want their children to have every privilege. But at the same time they are opposed to privilege for anyone else's children. They desire equal opportunity for everyone else's children, extra for their own. By standing for the general interest, the State therefore commands some support to uphold it against the bitter opposition which it provokes. Up till a few years ago, the general view amongst intelligent people was that the State had performed with admirable effect its functions of policing the family, so as to prevent it from having any undue influence on the occupational system. We underestimated the resistance of the family. The home is still the most fertile seed-bed of reaction.

My purpose at this point is not so much to review the recent evidence of family discontent as to outline its historical background. My intent is to stress that, despite the manifold changes of the last centuries, the family is still much the same kind of institution, inspired more by loyalty than reason, that it used to be in feudal times.

4. SPUR OF FOREIGN COMPETITION

Historical analysis indicates the inevitability of family opposition to progress; also the necessity of the meritocracy. The aristocracy and the family – twin springs of inertia – have not, we know, managed to stop social progress. The reason is simple: that Britain has had to vie with other nations in a competitive world. If it had not been for the spur of international rivalry, the internal society would not have become more vigorous; competitive selection in the civil service would never have become the exemplar for the nation as a whole.

The wars of the last century, as the apotheosis of

international competition, were also the great forcing-house for merit. At the time people used to say that in war there were no victors; victor and vanquished, all suffered alike. In the perspective of history we can see how untrue this was. Before nuclear fission arrived, war benefited everyone, especially the defeated countries – witness Russia, Germany, China. War stimulated invention, and, even more important, war stimulated the better use of human resources. In the First World War the U.S. Army put two million recruits through intelligence tests,[1] so successfully that practically all armies adopted the same practice when they were mobilized on later occasions. In the Second World War the British Army again demonstrated the extraordinary effectiveness of psychological selection. These were in their time great achievements. War woke people up to the fact that the nation possessed a supply of ability never ordinarily used to the full. Every child from an elementary school who became an officer in the Hitler war – many as they were, once merit rather than parentage became the test – was an argument for educational reform. It was no accident that the three great education Acts of the first half-century, in 1902, 1918, and

1. The directive setting out the objectives the U.S. Army wished to achieve has an air of extraordinary prescience about it. The test was to 'designate and select men whose superior intelligence indicated the desirability of advancement or special assignment; to select and recommend for "development battalions" such men as were so inferior intellectually as to be unsuited for regular military training; to enable officers to build up organizations of uniform mental strength, or in accordance with definite specifications concerning intellectual requirements; to select men for various types of military duty or for special assignments; to eliminate men whose intelligence was so inferior as to make it impossible to use them at all.' Quoted Eysenck, H. J. *Uses and Abuses of Psychology*. 1953.

1944, were put on the statute book at the end of the three wars, nor that the cause of reform, in civil service and army alike, was in the previous century so strongly assisted by the Crimea.

Competition with other countries was the pacemaker of peacetime too. The Englishman was made to fear that his effortless superiority might be a contradiction in terms: above the cosiness of Lords, the exclusiveness of Ascot, and the somnolence of the Federation of British Industries loomed the shadow of the clever foreigner. This internal class system was eventually changed by the international class system with which Englishmen were likewise obsessed – for ever discussing whether their country was a first-class power, or (after some setback) second-class, third-class, or no class at all. At the beginning of the last century the fear was of Germany; in the middle years, of American and, even more, of Russian competition; at the end, of Chinese.[1] At each stage the threat of the other country's armaments, the other country's trade and, more and more, the threat of the other country's science, was used to batter down resistance to change. It was always a question of quality. The other countries had chosen better raw material and, by better training, had produced from it better aeronauts, better physicists, better administrators, and, above all, better applied scientists. If Britain did not do likewise she was inviting defeat either in war or in trade; the recurring crises in the balance of payments made the second seem almost as deadly a threat as the first. For the sake of survival, the country *had* to meet the challenge of other countries less

1. The battle in the 1990s against making Chinese the second language in schools was an interesting example of continuing conservatism in a profession whose primary role is discouraging it.

hampered by rural ideas; which had benefited from more thorough social revolutions; which were not handicapped by island-psychology. Britain survived so long because it had repeated blood-transfusions from Australia, New Zealand, South Africa, and Canada, countries less handicapped by inheritance, who sent their talent to their mother-country. This could not go on for ever, and in science, if not in the arts, the supply from the Commonwealth began to dry up after 1945.

On this issue many old warnings are still most moving. The doughty Mr Forster, when introducing the first great Education Bill, on 17 February 1870, said:

We must not delay. Upon the speedy provision of elementary education depends our industrial prosperity. It is of no use trying to give technical teaching to our artisans without elementary education; uneducated labourers – and many of our labourers are utterly uneducated – are for the most part, unskilled labourers, and if we leave our workfolk any longer unskilled, notwithstanding their strong sinews and determined energy, they will become over-matched in the competition of the world. . . . If we are to hold our position among men of our own race or among the nations of the world we must make up the smallness of our numbers by increasing the intellectual force of the individual.[1]

Nearly a century later, Forster was echoed by the last but one of the great aristocrats in government.

In the last ten years, said Sir Winston Churchill, *the Soviet higher technical education for mechanical engineering has been developed both in numbers and quality to an extent which far*

1. Hansard, 17 February 1870. Quoted in *English Historical Documents* XII (1). Ed. Young, G. M., and Handcock, W. D., p. 914.

*exceeds anything we have achieved. This is a matter which needs
the immediate attention of Her Majesty's Government . . . if we
are – not to keep abreast – but even to maintain our porportion-
ate place in the world.*[1]

The reasons for the sorry state to which Sir Winston
referred were that higher education was too limited and
enjoyed by the wrong people. In 1945 as many as half
of the small number of students at the universities did
not have an adequate intelligence at all. 'At present
rather less than two per cent of the population reach the
Universities. About five per cent of the whole population show, on test, an intelligence as great as the upper
half of the students, who amount to one per cent of the
population.'[2] Ten years later many able working-class
children were still not getting to universities at all.[3] So
little intelligence at the universities! Many able people
not getting there at all! No wonder the annual productivity increment in the thirty years after 1945 was
only three per cent! No wonder the famous Ministry of
Education report on *Early Leaving* lamented the mass of
'wasted academic ability' which was squandered on
mere manual jobs instead of being cultivated in the

1. Reported in *The Times*, 6 December 1955. At that time Great
Britain was producing fewer graduates in engineering and other
applied sciences than almost any other major country. 2,800 a
year, or 57 per million of population, in Britain; compared with
22,000, or 136 per million, in U.S.A.; and 60,000, or 280 per
million, in the U.S.S.R. France was producing 70 per million,
Western Germany 86 per million, and Switzerland 82 per million.
See *Technical Education*, 1956. H.M.S.O. Cmd. 9703.

2. Barlow Report on Scientific Manpower. May 1946. H.M.S.O.
Cmd. 6824.

3. Report on university education published for the Committee
of Vice-Chancellors and Principals by the Association of Universities of the British Commonwealth, 1957.

grammar schools. Fortunately, the danger of being 'over-matched in the competition of the world' was so real and was stressed so vigorously in the last half of the century, the need to subordinate everything else to the claims of production so pressing, that education was at last decisively reformed and the family torn away from the feudal embrace.

Or so we thought.

5. SOCIALIST MIDWIVES

Progress would have been forfeit had it not been for the relentless efforts of the now famous 'midwives of progress'. The socialists accelerated the growth of large-scale organizations, and, unlike small businesses, these encouraged promotion by merit.[1] The Coal Board was in its own way as influential as the civil service. The socialists attacked all family influence and job succession. Labour pamphlets in the 1920s and 1930s (many of them republished in Harvard Socialist Documents) made a practice of ridiculing the current criterion of success – 'it's not what you know but who you know that counts'. They denounced inheritance of property. Death duties were not their triumph alone but it was they who so powerfully nourished the moral conviction that the children of rich parents should never receive advantage denied to the children of poor. For many

1. Large enterprises also needed more educated people. In 1930 the Metropolitan-Vickers Electrical Company, to take an example, employed some 10,000 people of whom nearly 2,000 required some form of organized education. In 1956 the company had 25,000 employees of whom 16,000 had to have some organized education. By 1982 61,000 out of a total of 74,000 had education up to the standard of Higher National Certificate, as it was then called. *Times Educational Supplement*, 17 February 1956.

years parents dodged death duties (the duties having to be avoided because the occasion could not be) by giving away much of their property before they died. The socialists eventually stopped this evasion by the first of their capital levies. Even these successes pale by the side of their greatest achievement – the progressive and fundamental improvement of the educational system. Pressure for greater equality of opportunity was unceasing, and as a result elementary schools were improved, secondary education made free, and the number of university scholarships multiplied. Although the Education Act of 1944 was introduced by a Conservative Minister in a Coalition Government, the purpose was that of the Labour Party. After that Act children were educated according to their 'age, ability, and aptitude', those with greater ability getting more education.

All in all, the British socialists of the first three-quarters of the last century (like Saint-Simon and his followers in France 200 years ago) were most commendable for the single-mindedness with which they attacked the evils of inheritance in property, job, and education. In so far as they were opposed to inequality it was to the kinds flowing from inheritance, and the form of equality they fostered most was in the truly vital theatre of opportunity. It is all very well for our modern feminists to say that in their discrimination they do not count these men as socialists; history is always being rewritten, but to carry conviction it needs to be done with more finesse than that. The socialists were the men who produced a new mental climate within the span of less than a century.

The greatest of their intellectual leaders did more than elaborate a critique of inheritance. The Morrises,

Tawneys, and Coles quaintly spoke of the 'dignity of labour' as though manual and mental work were of equal worth; overshadowing them, the greatest of the Fabians saw a vision of the new social order which would rise, on the foundation of human ability, from the unplanned chaos of the old. When they struck, they indeed struck hard. The tiny Fabian Society had galvanized the unthinking masses of Labour; so would the élite of the future inspire and direct the unthinking masses of the great society. Echoing Plato and Aristotle, Wells in *The Modern Utopia* conceived the brilliant notion of the Samurai; the rulers whom no power corrupts, as wise as they were disinterested. The Webbs went further and discovered the Order of the Samurai incarnate in the Vocation of Leadership of the Soviet Communist Party. The Webbs have an honoured place today because they saw that in the Soviet Union, though marred both then and for many years after by the forms of a quite unnecessary *political* dictatorship, a dedicated, disciplined, and above all educated minority were chosen primarily for their ability, and that this minority exercised, with a success which history confirms, that 'leadership without which democracy, in any of its forms, is but a mob'.[1] Shaw himself described the goal with characteristic pungency.

This haphazard Mobocracy, he cried, *must be replaced by democratic aristocracy: that is, by the dictatorship, not of the whole proletariat, but of that five per cent of it capable of conceiving the job and pioneering in the drive towards its divine goal.*[2]

1. Webb, S. and B. *Soviet Communism – A New Civilization.* Longmans, 1935.
2. *Fabian Essays.* Postscript to 1948 Edition on 'Sixty Years of Fabianism'.

In his great *Everybody's Political What's What?*[1] Shaw elaborated this plea so strikingly that it is still read to-day by serious students of social thought.

6. SUMMARY

This sketch of the social forces which have shaped our time is familiar enough. We should hardly need reminding that progress has ever been born of conflict. The monarchy, the aristocracy, and the gentry, all the things that went with our agricultural past, were too long held in reverence; and as a result the family, always conservative in its influence, was so buttressed by the feudal tradition as to uphold inheritance, of wealth, of job, and above all, of prestige, long after the claims of efficiency had been more fully recognized in other countries. These forces on the one side only yielded after a long struggle to superior strength on the other. The necessity to withstand international competition in peace and war was borne home upon all the most intelligent people; and the Labour Party, expressing the grievances of those with nothing to inherit or bequeath, drew up the masses in good order behind the more far-sighted leaders of all political persuasions.

1. See, for instance, pp. 345 ff., 1944.

CHAPTER TWO

THREAT OF COMPREHENSIVE SCHOOLS

I. THIRD FORCE IN THE SCHOOLS

THE last century was still bent upon the conquest of Nature. What vanity this now seems! Science penetrates her secrets not for the sake of human dominance (illusory as this always is) but in order to discover the laws which man must *obey*. The highest fulfilment lies in submission. Of nothing is this more true than of society; and here no lesson has been more simple, and yet more painful than the fact of genetic inequality. The condition of progress is submission to the frugality of Nature. For every man enlivened by excellence, ten are deadened by mediocrity, and the object of good government is to ensure that the latter do not usurp the place in the social order which should belong to their betters. Of one method by which this has been done I have already spoken – it was by weakening the power of the family. The other complementary method of advance, to which I now turn, has been to enhance the influence of the school.

I have, in the previous chapter, given the Labour Party due credit for the truly vital part it played in undermining the old hereditary system. I must now, in order to redress the balance, explain that in the middle of the century the Party changed its clothes. Previously Labour, with support from low-caste ability, stood for progress against the high-caste leadership of the Conservatives. Then the two changed sides, and the Conservatives, with the new meritocracy growing in strength behind them, came to represent progress (up till just recently, that is) against socialists who obstinately persisted in their increasingly irrelevant attachment to egalitarianism. I do not mean to castigate the whole Labour Party. At no time did the left-wing champions of comprehensive schools command a firm and consistent majority in the counsels of the Party. They had a substantial influence all the same, and until their campaign fizzled out, the educational reforms, which I will briefly relate in this chapter, could not be completed.

Till the middle of the century practical socialists identified equality with advancement for merit. The trouble started when the left wing emphasized a different interpretation of equality, and, ignoring differences in human ability, urged that everyone, those with talent as well as those without, should attend the same schools and receive the same basic education. The issue attained extraordinary prominence in the political controversies of the 1960s and 1970s. Dr Nightingale has shown in his *Social Origins of the Comprehensive Schools* that the movement was inspired very largely by sentimental egalitarianism of the modern sort, far removed from the hard-headed realism of Bernard Shaw, and it is this which constitutes its significance for us today. The extremists used every argument that came to hand. The future development of children could not be accurately assessed at the tender age of eleven. The strain upon parents and children of the competitive examination was too great. Once children were shepherded into separate pens it was too difficult for those who developed late to transfer from one to another. Their chief interest was not, however, so much educational as social; the left-wingers claimed that to segregate the clever from the stupid was to deepen class divisions. They proposed that all children, irrespective of sex, race, creed, class (that was all right but they went on), *or* ability, should be lumped together.

The long debate was never purely domestic in scope. International competition between economies was also competition between schools; as this truth became truism, people became almost as interested in foreign techniques of education as in foreign techniques of production. Especially the socialists. Which countries, they rhetorically asked, have the highest productivity? Are not these the same countries that have comprehensive schools – Australia, New Zealand, Scotland, Sweden, Canada, above all, Russia and America? Is not the moral obvious, that the battle for production will be won on the playing-fields of the common schools? Here, with all its habitual appeal, was the old and fallacious argument by analogy.

English socialists were slow to appreciate the force of the transatlantic model: America, they thought, could not be socialist because it had no socialist movement. But they eventually woke up to the fact that the country had no socialist movement for a different reason, because in essentials it was already socialist. They then hailed the United States as the nearest thing on earth to a classless society,[1] and, their prejudices being what they were, naturally turned truth upside down by attributing responsibility for this remarkable phenomenon to the comprehensive high schools. Practically all American children attended these as a matter of course before so many rich parents began to patronize the private

1. One of the first indications of this change was the influential book, *The Future of Socialism*, written by the young Mr C. A. R. Crosland in 1956.

schools which expanded in the U.S.A. at the same time as they contracted in Britain. It is easy to see why English left-wingers had such sympathy for their American brothers. Their underlying attitudes were so much alike. The dispossessed emigrants who set the tone of American society were in revolt against the patronizing airs of European snobbery; so were the underprivileged socialists of Britain. Americans, far from prizing brain-power, despised it, despised it because they feared the claims of intellect as the most wounding of all. So did many of the socialists. The distinction of the Americans was that they put their beliefs into practice. In the continent of the common man they established common schools which recognized no child superior to another. Whatever their name, tongue, race, or religion, and whatever their talent, all children were subject to the same 'education' in the same high schools. What the socialists did not permit themselves to recognize was the reason for this success. The socialists could not understand the reasons why the tree could not be transplanted. They could not understand that in America common schools were needed, in a way they were never needed in Europe, to wrest nationhood from polyglot chaos. The restless were responding to an inner necessity of their society far more compelling than in Britain when they professed that:

We hold these truths to be self-evident, that all men are created equal, that they are endowed by their Creator with certain inalienable rights, that among these are life, liberty, the the pursuit of happiness, and a high school diploma.[1]

Vaunting American comprehensive schools, a tonic

1. Quoted by Richmond, W. K. *Education in the United States.* 1956.

to the apostles, only confirmed the opposition of more right-thinking people. American education was notorious for low standards. Age for age, the British child was invariably better educated; grammar schools were superior in scholarship to American colleges, and as for comparing Manchester University, say, with Kansas State College! What could be expected when schools were treated as institutions not for education but for social levelling? The left-wingers did no good to their cause by drawing so much attention to America; the model was of what not to do.

The enthusiasts had a last trump to play – the Soviet Union. Political antipathies were for many years so strong, that to say that any institution existed in Russia was enough to condemn it. The mood began to change in the late 1950s. When travel to the U.S.S.R. was permitted, visitors reported[1] that comprehensive schools were to be spied there too; and what's more, free from some of the defects of the American ones. All Soviet children attended the same Middle Schools from seven until seventeen, without selection and without streaming. But the Russians had good teachers, relatively far better-paid than America, the children were more disciplined, had to work harder, and were not given the same absurd multiplicity of choice of subjects. Academic standards were a good deal higher than in the other United States. In 1957, at the time of the first Sputnik,

1. An early instance was the report on *Education in the Soviet Union* published by The Educational Interchange Council in 1957. See p. 4. 'With the exception of a limited number of educationally sub-normal children, all go to the same school . . . within the same school any attempt to stream children according to their ability is strictly forbidden. The dullest child works side by side with the ablest in the same classroom and keeps pace as best he can.'

a U.S. Government report admitted that the Russian adolescent had a better grounding in mathematics, physics, and chemistry, and in the humanities too, than his American counterpart. All the same, standards were certainly not so high as in the better English grammar schools. Refusal to segregate the able from the stupid meant that there was no sixth-form work of the type which has always been the pride of the better sort of school in England.

The left-wing socialists were shrewd enough to know the best colours to fly in a Britain at long last becoming aware of its economic backwardness. They praised America and Russia for their efficiency and claimed that high schools were responsible. In fact the truth was the other way round – the United States of East and West could afford to waste human talent, yet still fare well in international competition, just because they were relatively so rich in other resources of Nature. Like each other in so many ways, both countries also compensated for absence of competition in the schools by pressing it home afterwards. Russian universities only admitted the best candidates after a stiff examination, which incidentally kept standards up in the Middle Schools; the businessmen of America did their best to make up for the deficiencies of the educational system by selecting the most able after they became adults. In Britain competition was at school, in America after. But detailed social research in the 1960s showed that neither Russian universities nor American businessmen could overcome the initial handicap imposed by the common schools. Not even the virtuoso could make up later for the years wasted in childhood being treated as though he were an ordinary person. Exceptional brains require exceptional teaching: Russians and Americans could not see it. They forced every child to do what he was not good at as well as what he was. By showing that all men are equally duffers at something – what could be more easy? – they went as far as they could to show that no man is a genius at anything – what could be more dangerous? In the name of equality they wantonly sacrificed the few to the many.

The debate jogged on until the 1980s, when the socialists were for once silenced by the facts. In that decade our modern notions passed the acid test of productivity. Thanks in part to atomic power which released Britain from dependence on oil and coal, in part to the economic advantages of European unification; but thanks mainly to the scientific management of talent, in productivity little Britain began to leave the giants behind. The 1944 Education Act began to tell, and our country has continued to forge ahead ever since. From being first with the Industrial Revolution of the nineteenth century, Britain became first in the intellectual revolution of the twentieth. The workshop of the world became the grammar school of the world.

2. AGITATION DEFEATED

To us the failure of comprehensive schools does not seem to require explanation. We can hardly conceive of a society built upon consideration for the individual regardless of his merit, regardless of the needs of society as a whole. But as students of historical sociology, we must always try to understand the events of the past, not as we see them, but as the people of the time used to see them. We have to try to think ourselves into their minds in the social situations which confronted *them*. If we do this, we are bound to recognize that the left-wing socialists did have a chance. The 1960s and 1970s were their historic moment. The hereditary class system of birth and wealth was crumbling fast. People were unsure of their values, even doubting whether there was any such thing as progress, and as always when people are unsure they were gullible. They were told that in a classless society they would feel safe again, the comprehensive school the ship that would sail them home. Had there been nothing to the movement except wishy-washy idealism, then of course it would have evaporated harmlessly in a hundred summer schools. As it was, the leaders actually had followers. The idealists were backed by the discontented, people who had suffered from the judgement of educational selection, and were just intelligent enough to be able to focus their resentment on some limited grievance, the streaming of infant schools, the eleven plus exam, the smaller classes in grammar schools, or whatever it might happen to be. They were backed by parents whose children were allotted, in all fairness in everyone's eyes except their own, to secondary modern schools; and by frustrated adults who blamed their own schooling for later disappointments, and wanted to deprive others too of the chances which they felt they themselves had missed. It was a motley band, yet as always when intellectual idealism chimes with lumpen frustration, it was formidable. We therefore need to turn the question around, and ask – why, with these assets, did the movement not after all succeed?

I spoke in the last chapter of the evils of the aristocratic embrace – of all the cheap imitations of the image of nobility enshrined in the popular mind. Britain suffered sorely from a caste snobbery planted too deeply in the national character for anything but a social revolution on the American or Russian scale to eradicate. If

this was our curse, and curse it was, it was also our blessing. This great paradox is the clue to Britain's social
history. In our island we never discarded the values of
the aristocracy, because we never discarded the aristocracy. It displayed an amazing resilience which allowed
it, as so often in previous centuries, to disappoint the
many critics waiting to attend its funeral. Its institutions, the monarchy, the peerage, the ancient universities, and the public schools, adapted slowly but all the
more surely to the changing needs of a changing society,
which therefore remained in a fundamental sense hierarchical. Englishmen of the solid centre never believed
in equality. They assumed that some men were better
than others, and only waited to be told in what respect.
Equality? Why, there would be no one to look up to any
more. Most Englishmen believed, however dimly, in a
vision of excellence which was part and parcel of their
own time-honoured aristocratic tradition. It was because of this that the campaign for comprehensive
schools failed. It was because of this that we have
our modern society: by imperceptible degrees an
aristocracy of birth has turned into an aristocracy of
talent.

All depended upon timely educational reform. In the
nineteenth century this was delayed too long. If the
Education Act of 1871 had come fifty years earlier
there would perhaps have been no Chartism; had the
1902 Act coincided with the Great Exhibition, no
Labour Party. Sir Keir Hardie would have gone from a
secondary school to the Board of Education, and Bishop
Arthur Henderson would have watched over the
finances of the Ecclesiastical Commission. Wise rulers
know that the best way to defeat opposition is to win
over its leaders; England was slow to learn that, in an

industrial society, this means appropriating and educating the able children of the lower classes while they are still young. But eventually the rulers did learn; in a competitive world they had to. To such effect that by the last quarter of the century the Labour extremists were fatally weakened. Since the ablest children were already in the grammar schools, their parents had the stoutest of stakes both in the existing educational system and in the existing social order. Their proxy place in the hierarchy made them deaf to the heralds of the common school.

Opposition from parents, teachers, and children – from the whole grammar stream in society – was the main reason for the failure of the comprehensive schools. These were not conceived as an entirely new kind of school – when it came to detailed planning the American model was fortunately forgotten. Their advocates realized well enough that some children were brighter than others. Yet at the same time they wanted children of grammar-school ability to walk beside their inferiors in a deceit of equality. For the full success of their plans, they needed to combine grammar schools with secondary modern. About the latter there was no problem; their status could only be raised by unification. Grammar schools were in a quite different state: they had nothing to gain, and almost everything to lose, by the change. This hard fact daunted the most resolute of Labour Education Committees, and some of them were certainly determined. But they were up against grammar-school masters who knew that Labour aspirations were simply impractical, and, to the country's undying credit, this has usually been sufficient to condemn anything. One of the great High Masters of Manchester Grammar School, writing as early as 1951, put

the issue as succinctly as it could be put today. The
Professor Conant of whom he speaks was an American
Professor apparently well known at the time – he illus-
trates again the intrusion of the United States into our
domestic forum.

*When Professor Conant demands 'a common core of general
education which will unite in one cultural pattern the future carpenter, factory worker, bishop, lawyer, doctor, sales-manager,
professor, and garage mechanic', he is simply asking for the
impossible. The demand for such a common culture rests either
on an altogether over-optimistic belief in the educability of the
majority that is certainly not justified by experience or on a
willingness to surrender the highest standards of taste and judgement to the incessant demands of mediocrity.*[1]

There might have been a different outcome had the
country's population been growing fast, as it was in the
United States when their high schools were established;
then the authorities could have issued a fiat that *new*
schools should be comprehensive, instead of grammar.
But with relative stability of population, not many new
grammar schools were built. What was the purpose of
having many more when even the existing grammar
schools could not get as many able children as they
could accommodate? As it was, comprehensive schools
were largely confined to Labour strongholds whose
population was expanding fast, to a few rural areas
which could not afford a complete range of schools, and
to places where a badly-housed second-rate grammar
school was ready to amalgamate in return for favours
from the authorities.

Though such comprehensive schools as were started –

1. James, E. *Education for Leadership*. 1951.

there was a small wave of them in the 1960s – must by the verdict of history be judged retrogressive, they were not nearly so dangerous as some of the socialist threats portended. In a hierarchical system like ours every institution has always modelled itself on the one immediately superior, which has usually meant the older – the new professions on the old, the modern universities on the ancient, and the comprehensive schools on the grammar. The planners were (happily for posterity) terrified by the kind of criticism fired at them by the grammar schools, and did their best to show it baseless. They imported old principles into new framework and made the core of the comprehensive not so much a common curriculum as a miniature grammar school. They made a grammar school first and added on the other bits later. To justify having a sixth-form of grammar size they were even prepared to make the whole school much larger than it otherwise need be – some of the early comprehensives actually had more than 2,000 in a veritable city of children. The interests of the clever children came first, or at least were not ignored. Obviously it would have been wrong to place the bright children in the same class as the dull, for then the former would have been held back to the pace of the slowest. In practice, the comprehensive schools, by dividing the goats from the sheep, continued to abide by the segregation of ability which was the saving grace of the whole educational system. More intelligent children continued in the main to get higher standard teaching not so much inferior to that which they would have obtained in a grammar school proper. This much is clear from some eye-witness accounts of the early comprehensive schools in action. One survey in the 1950s (by a Mr Pedley) said that:

with the opening in September 1953 of a new school at Llan-gefni, Anglesey completed its provision of comprehensive second-dary schools for the island, and was able to abandon its selection examination. But one of the first steps of the heads of the two comprehensive schools visited was to arrange internal tests for the newly-arrived pupils; and on the basis of what these revealed, together with junior school records, to grade the pupils in order of ability. Nor were Anglesey and the Isle of Man unusual in adopting this attitude. The five 'interim-compre-hensive' schools which I saw in London, and other schools in Middlesex and Walsall, all used the external examination test to assist them in classifying incoming pupils.[1]

Even though comprehensive schools had grammar streams they were unable to persuade parents with clever children to regard them with favour. Given a choice, parents naturally plumped for the grammar school proper, rather than for its less venerable imita-tion. In the long run ambitious parents always brought to grief the best-laid schemes of egalitarian reformers.

3. THE LEICESTER HYBRID

When it became apparent that the new schools were not satisfying the hopes of their champions, a sect within the socialist movement changed its tactics, and put forward another demand. The primary schools were at that time common schools for children of all grades of ability. So why not extend a kind of primary school to include all children up to fourteen or fifteen, as well as below eleven? The American high schools had originally been a kind of projection of the elementary; let Britain fol-low. All children would then go at eleven to a high school, and only later to a grammar school.

1. Pedley, R. *Comprehensive Schools Today*. 1954.

The proposal had several advantages.[1] Politically, it was far more acceptable because it did not seem to suggest a radical change, and, as I have said, the best way to do anything new in England was to pretend that it was not. The common school was merely to be projected forward instead of built afresh, the grammar schools preserved. This reform would also have either abolished or postponed selection for the grammar school and so avoided the undesirable strains of the existing eleven plus examination upon parents and children (including those who would not anyhow stay at school beyond the minimum age).

An experiment of this kind was in fact tried out by the Leicestershire County Council,[2] and many variations of it were later adopted by other education authorities. Why did not this movement carry all before it? The reasons are again illuminating. The educational reforms of the last century, being superimposed upon a hierarchical society, stood or fell by the success with which they enabled the clever child to leave the lower class into which he was born and to enter the higher class into which he was fitted to climb. English schools too had a vital social function, though a different one from the American. The educational ladder was also a social ladder – the scruffy, ill-mannered boy who started at five years old at the bottom had to be metamorphosed, rung by rung, into a more presentable, more polished, and more confident as well as a more knowledgeable lad at the top. He had to acquire a new accent – the most indelible mark of class in England –

1. An early version was put forward by the Croydon Education Committee, and ably amplified by Pedley, R., in *Comprehensive Education*, 1956.

2. See *The Leicestershire Experiment*. Stewart C. Mason. 1957.

and to any but the most determined man, that was well-nigh impossible unless he started young. When he finished his climb, he could then stand comparison with others who had begun their ascent from a much higher level. The social ladder was so long – the gap between the styles of life of upper and lower classes so wide – that promising children had to begin their climb through the schools at the earliest age possible. Postponing social assimilation until eleven was bad enough. If clever low-class children had not been able to move in the more stimulating atmosphere of the grammar schools, alongside many of the same age from higher classes, until they were sixteen, some of them would then have been too old ever to shake off their origins and so overcome their handicap. The schools would then have failed to fulfil one of their essential purposes in a progressive class system; they would not have been society's escalators for the gifted.

The second reason for rejection of selection at fifteen was that, as educators realized full well, clever children had to be caught young if they were to achieve, as adults, the highest standards of which they were capable and with the growth in complexity of science and technology only the highest standards were high enough. Scientists, whose best work is often done before they are thirty, need from the earliest possible years to get an intensive education of the sort that few Americans[1] have been able to get since high schools came into vogue, and

1. One absurdity of the American university system in particular, until 1986, was that so many good students, instead of getting adequate scholarships, had to work not at acquiring knowledge, but at washing dishes. They had to 'work' their way through college by not working at the purpose for which the institution ostensibly existed. *Per ardua ad inferna!*

Benjamin Franklin out. If the start of serious work were delayed till sixteen, and meanwhile they were being taught in a high school which could never attract staff as good as the grammar schools, they might not finish their education in time to take advantage of the few really fruitful years allowed by Nature. The grammar schools were responsible for Britain's fame in pure science even before Queen Elizabeth II came to the throne. Lord Cholmondeley has shown that, taking the last century as a whole, the number of fundamental discoveries was in relation to its population 2·3 times larger than Germany, 4·3 times larger than the U.S.A., and 5·1 times larger than the U.S.S.R. Would cosmic radiation have been understood without Simon? Distant stellar exploration possible without Bird himself? The south-western counties concreted over and reserved for cars without Piper? Babies ever carried safely at a speed of Mach 102 without Percy? But for the grammar school might not all these great men have been shopkeepers and mechanics? Pity was that until the end of the century Britain's science was nowhere near matched by its achievement in technology. Still, it is a proud record, and would have been forfeit to the 'incessant demands of mediocrity' had common uneducation persisted into adolescence.

4. SUMMARY

Before the schools could evolve into the modern system described in the next chapter, the threat from the left had to be warded off. Socialists who wanted all children, regardless of their ability, educated as in America and Russia, commanded enough popular support for a time to convert what should have been a purely educational question into a major political issue. Yet they were bound to fail. To succeed with education they needed a social revolution which would overthrow the established hierarchy, values, and all. But with the masses dormant and their potential leaders diverted into self-advancement, what hope was there? Grammar schools remained. Comprehensive schools withered. Even the Leicester hybrid never bloomed. The vandals were vanquished and the city stood.

CHAPTER THREE

ORIGINS OF MODERN EDUCATION

I. THE MOST FUNDAMENTAL REFORM

ONCE general opinion, even in the Labour Party, turned against comprehensive schools, it became possible to concentrate upon the most fundamental of reforms, that is, upon the all-round improvement of grammar schools. Above all they needed more money, more money to retain their best scholars, and more money for the teachers.

The Hitler war transformed the social composition of these schools. Full employment and larger wages, fostering higher aspirations, made lower-class parents able and anxious to get better education for their children, and the 1944 Act[1] helped by making secondary schools free. The consequences were dramatic. In the 1930s only a minority of able low-class children had more than the most primitive education; twenty years later practically all clever children were installed in the seats of learning. A sociological study of the 1950s was able to report that 'in very many, if not in most, parts of the country the chances of children at a given level of ability entering grammar schools are no longer dependent on their social origins'.[2]

However, it was one thing for able children from the

1. The date has perhaps been given an importance beyond its deserts by the tendency of schoolmasters to teach history by its important dates – 1870, 1902, 1918, 1944, 1972, and so forth.

2. Floud, J. E., Halsey, A. H., and Martin, F. M. *Social Class and Educational Opportunity.* 1956.

lower classes to enter grammar schools, another for them to stay there. Here prosperity was a handicap. Even against the wishes of their parents, many scholars were tempted by high wages to leave school early – and flocks of them did so at the minimum age.[1] Prosperity did not create the problem, but it accentuated one of long-standing. In every decade children matured physically earlier than before. Constant shortening of childhood in the biological and social sense and constant lengthening of childhood in the educational sense posed a dilemma which was only resolved in the long run by treating grammar-school children as adults.

The superior classes took for granted that their children should enjoy higher education; the difficulty was not to get the able to stay at school, but to get the stupid to leave and put up with the manual jobs for which their intelligence fitted them. In the lower classes the situation was reversed. The higher the wages that could be earned at a machine by the children of manual workers, the more dreary seemed the school-desk. No age is more acquisitive than adolescence. The remedy was clear: the State had to prevent children from suffering for their cleverness by giving them and their parents a privileged status within the lower classes. The first step was to pay very much larger maintenance allowances – later scaled in ratio to intelligence – for grammar-school children staying the full course. But this was not enough. Inquiry showed that some irresponsible parents were spending the allowances on themselves, not on the children for whom they were intended. The obvious thing to do –

1. In the early 1950s very many of the grammar-school boys capable of finishing the course left before doing so, and most of these were the children of manual workers. See *Early Leaving*, published by the Ministry of Education in 1954.

eventually even to Ministers of Education – was to pay a learning wage direct to grammar-school pupils. At first it was equal to the average earnings of juveniles in ordinary industry; then the newly formed B.U.G.S.A. (the British Union of Grammar School Attenders) attacked the injustice of equality, rightly too, since the ability of the earner was usually so much lower than that of the pupil. In 1972 the government approved a learning wage on a sliding scale sixty per cent above industrial earnings. After that very few children left grammar schools prematurely for economic reasons. In modern times we could hardly imagine a grammar school without its weekly pay-day.

The universities paid wages to students (in the form of scholarships) long before grammar schools, but other-wise preserved some curious anachronisms of their own. Poorer parents were at a disadvantage in grammar schools, richer parents in universities. In the 1950s clever children of the middle-rich were deprived of grants because their parents were quite wrongly sup-posed to have enough money to pay, with the shocking result that some of them never got to university at all – surely a supreme example of the excesses of egalitarianism in its heyday! Closed 'scholarships' also gave pupils from certain public schools privileged entry to otherwise reputable colleges at Oxford and Cambridge; and in the middle of the century it was still not unknown for King's or Balliol to detect some special merit in sons whose fathers had been there before. Such barbaric practices were even excused in public from time to time by old-fashioned dons who declared it was better, educationally mind you, for the bright students to be mixed up with the dull. The dons had once again lost touch: the modern world no longer required the clever to mingle with the stupid, except when assigned to social intelligence work among the lower classes. When the die-hards died, universities came into line with national policy and selected all their entrants on merit properly tested in the examination-room. By 1972 public school-boys had either to compete openly with the Bradford Grammar School or seek 'gringo admission' to South American universities. Few willingly incurred that stigma.

2. HIGHER SALARIES FOR TEACHERS

The learning wage and the universalization of university scholarships followed upon a change in the attitude of the State to spending on education, which itself reflected growing recognition that investment in brains is much more rewarding than investment in property. But politicians always wanted the impossible – the quick results education can never give. They kept tinkering with the top of the educational system instead of building securely from the bottom. They were as willing to spend on the universities as they were unwilling to spend on the primary schools. Politicians would not realize that the milk monitors were the future leaders of the nation. Faced with a shortage of engineers, the government said very well, spend more upon the engineering colleges. Of scientists, spend more upon the science faculties. Of technologists generally, then build more schools of technology. This was futile. For if the government attracted more promising youngsters into engineering, fewer were left behind for science. More for the civil service meant less for industry, more for laboratories less for teaching. The egalitarian doctrine that any man can be trained to substitute for any other was so deeply rooted that our ancestors only slowly came to appreciate the full significance of one simple fact: that all the professions were competing with each other for a limited supply of intelligence. It was not until well on into the last half of the century that the national scarcity of intellect became obvious to all those who had it. The government learned that the only way simultaneously to get more and better engineers, more and better physicists, more and better civil servants up to the limits set by Nature was to start with the three-year-olds, to ensure that from that age on no ability escaped through the net, and, most important, to make certain that the future physicists, psychologists, and the rest of the élite continuously had the best teaching they could get.

It did not matter so much about the defective, maladjusted, and delinquent upon whom up to 1972 England (as a sign of the times) spent more than upon the brilliant. It did not matter so much about the secondary modern schools. In an ideal world, not hampered by shortage of resources, the unfortunate could have large sums spent on them too. But it was not, has not been, nor ever will be, an ideal world. The choice was between priorities, and there was no doubt how the decision had to go. What mattered most were primary schools, where the pupils were being divided into the gifted and the ungifted; and, above all, the grammar schools where the gifted received their due. They had to have more generous endowments. And they got them.

From the moment that Sir Anthony Crosland was persuaded that the battle for national survival would be won or lost in the 'A' streams all the way from nursery to grammar school, the money began to flow. Spending on education was still only 2·7 per cent of the gross national product in 1953;[1] by 1963, 3·9 per cent; by 1982, after the 'marvellous decade', it was 6·1 per cent. Most of the extra went on teachers. For more of them – it was still common in those grim middle years of the last century for one single teacher to have a mob of forty children in a class and who could she then be but a Joseph Lancaster![2] And for better ones. So far were teachers' salaries behind industry that in the early 1960s some grammar schools did not have a solitary physics teacher. At a time when the Atomic Energy Authority was clamouring for physicists! Many of the leading officials at the Ministry of Education and the Treasury, though they had read their Plato, had seemingly forgotten that none but the guardians themselves could be trusted to teach future guardians. Second-rate teachers, a second-rate élite: the meritocracy can never be better than its teachers. Things improved until at last the teachers attained their ideal of superiority of esteem. One of the wisest strokes of the marvellous decade was to put the salaries of science teachers on the same level as scientists in industry and all grammar-school teachers on the same level as their scientific colleagues. The schools could then attract good scientists; they got the very pick of other teachers.

1. This earlier figure was found in Wiles, P. J. D., *The Nation's Intellectual Investment*. (Bull. O. U. Inst. of Stats. August 1956, p. 279); the latter are from the ordinary, popular editions of *Education Statistics*.

2. 'We want ten, and by jingo we want to know when' was as effective a slogan, used in the campaign for raising the pupil-teacher ratio in grammar schools to 1/10, as the earlier slogan 'We want eight, and we won't wait', used in the campaign for more dreadnoughts. 'We want scholarships, not battleships', another. The Small Class was merely substituted for the Big Navy.

The logic of the system can be portrayed in a simple table.

Distribution of Intelligence between types of Secondary School (1989)

Type of school	I.Q. level of pupils	No. of pupils per teacher	I.Q. level of teachers
E.S.N. (Educationally Subnormal) School	50–80	25	100–105
Secondary modern	81–115	20	105–110
Secondary grammar	116–180	10	135–180
Boarding grammar	125–180	8	135–180

3. BOARDING GRAMMAR SCHOOLS

The movement for comprehensive schools did more than threaten standards in the grammar schools. If successful, it would have led to indefinite postponement of the quite vital reform of the public schools. Knowing that their children would get no better than a second-rate training in State schools, parents with the means to pay would never have been restrained from purchasing the advantages of private education; and equality of opportunity would have remained a dream.

The demise of the public school was freely prophesied between 1939 and 1945. It was feared that impoverishment of the middle classes would remove their capacity to pay fees, and some of the strongest supporters of the public schools looked to the State to prevent catastrophe. They were not only ready to accept a proportion of poor pupils, they pleaded with the State to pay for their places.[1] The future was not as expected – it

1. See the Fleming Report: *The Public Schools and the General Educational System.* 1944.

seldom is. The middle class proved as tough as ever; they survived high taxation and high prices and went on sending their children to the same old venerable schools. In the middle 1950s, of people with more than £1,000 p.a. – a miserable enough sum by modern standards – nineteen out of every twenty sent their children to private schools.[1] Incidentally, this included many 'socialists'. As Sir Hartley Shawcross said in 1956 – 'I do not know a single member of the Labour Party, who can afford to do so, who does not send his children to a public school, often at great sacrifice – not for snobbish reasons or to perpetuate class distinction, but to ensure his children get the best.'

Public-school pupils made up about a quarter of the sixth forms in all kinds of schools, State and private together. Since they paid more, on the whole they enjoyed a better education than their fellows in State schools. To judge from autobiographies and novels, there may have been some truth in the saying that at a public school the pupil was taught how to grow up into a boy, but, if so, at least he was an educated boy and therefore better fitted to take his place in a complex society than an uneducated man. There was no harm in the public schools imparting a superior education – it was all to the good; what was wrong was that the privileged were chosen by other criteria than merit. They were selected by their parents' bank accounts. They unashamedly inherited their education, and with it their future status in the society they should have been intent to serve.

How was such nepotism to be abolished? It was a long and bitter business, perhaps only paralleled by the

1. 'Savings and Finances of the Upper Income Classes'. Klein, L. R., Straw, K. H., Vandome, P. *Bulletin of Oxford Institution of Statistics*. November 1956.

crusade for the abolition of slavery in the previous century, and only successful because the energy which had been previously directed into comprehensive schools was diverted and harnessed to this more constructive task. Year by year, but especially in 1958, Labour Party statements said that 'Labour must no longer hesitate to tackle the greatest source of social inequality and class division in our society – the private schools.' But they did hesitate, even though the leaders of Labour were guilty public-school men themselves. The schools could not be effectively closed down or nationalized by decree; unless the parents had been forbidden to spend money on their children – itself too grave an interference with the family to be politically practical – they would have started up their own black-market establishments elsewhere. One Eton closed would have been another Eton opened. Parents had to be appeased as well as bullied. The 1958 declaration, *Learning to Live*, was most sensible and far-sighted when it said that:

Labour concludes that at present no scheme for 'taking over' or 'democratizing' the public schools shows sufficient merits to justify the large diversion of public money that would be involved. In time to come, when maintained schools are improved, when the prestige of the public schools is consequently diminished, and when substantial changes in the distribution of wealth and in public opinion have occurred, the question, in a changed form, will once more arise.

Final triumph was the result of an ingenious pincer-movement. Research showed that most of the fees for public schools were paid out of capital. The upper classes, for fear of the duties, very largely stopped passing money from one generation to another upon death. The established practice was for grandparents, while still alive, to transfer property not so much to their children as to their grandchildren for the purchase of a privileged education. Death duties were powerless to stop this kind of three-generation abuse, acted indeed as an incentive to it, and had to be supplemented by a series of capital levies. The sixth Labour Government, with Crosland and Hughes working as a team in the two key Ministries, initiated a great capital levy, and thenceforward the capital gains tax prevented the acquisition of new fortunes. The public schools felt the squeeze right away. The effect of the levy was somewhat offset by the growing inequality of earned incomes, but not so much as totally to defeat its object. Conditions were certainly harsher for the public schools in 1970 than they had been twenty years earlier.

Of greater importance than capital levy was the steady improvement in the standards of grammar schools themselves. It all came down, as I have said, to pounds, shillings, and pence. Why was Rugby superior to the Walsall Grammar School? It was quite simple, Rugby spent so much more per boy, therefore Rugby got better teachers and more teachers. When the money spent on Walsall was multiplied – a portion of the capital levy was earmarked for new grammar-school laboratories and other buildings – the quality of the school was improved out of all recognition. As long as the State could keep down total expenditure on public schools, and step up expenditure on its own schools, victory was in the long run assured. Parents besieged Walsall instead of Rugby, and found their children had to compete on level terms with all other children, none but the best being chosen. Only if their children were too stupid to gain entry to Walsall did they fall back on Rugby, which could hardly remain a first-rate school if its pupils were second-rate. The prestige balance between public and grammar was gradually, but decisively, tilted in the latter's favour.

Private schools did not have to be abolished; the best of them abolished themselves. Wide-awake public-school headmasters worried about the stupidity of the children they were attracting, and as the drift of events became clear, and as the Treasury became more open-handed, solved their problems by negotiating with the State for inclusion on the roll of 'grant-aided boarding grammar schools', as they were ponderously called in official language. For this enviable status to be secured they had to agree to take a majority of children chosen in the ordinary way by the local authorities from the primary schools. Eton in 1972 reduced its entrance age to eleven and undertook to accept eighty per cent of Queen's scholars, pushed home to one hundred per cent in 1991. Where Eton led, others followed.

Unless Her Majesty's Inspectors granted the school a certificate of efficiency, only done if academic standards were at least as high as in day grammar schools, it could not be admitted to the roll. All the better-known public schools – in fact nearly all associated with what was called the Headmasters' Conference – were in time admitted and thrown open to talented children who needed a boarding-school education for one good reason or another – say because they had no parents, or came from homes moved frequently, or because they lived in the countryside too far for daily attendance at an ordinary grammar school. Other private schools, the majority, were allowed to go their own way. Since they nurtured no first-rate brains, the State was not particularly concerned what went on behind their class-room doors – as long, that is, as they reached the minimum standards of hygiene and efficiency in practical crafts laid down for the modern schools to which ordinary run-of-the mill children were sent. Naturally enough, once the private schools were reserved for the mediocre, they no longer conferred any social *cachet* and the number of parents willing to waste their money on them diminished year by year. This was, of course, apart from the anthroposophists, diet reformers, and latter-day anarchists who clung obsessively to their own educational foundations.

The integration of the two types of grammar school led to many beneficial changes in the content of education. The day schools were famed for their healthy concentration on science; the best of them not only encouraged specialization in order to bestow intensive knowledge of at least one limited branch, what is far more important they bred that scientific attitude, precise, curious, speculative, sceptical, that humility towards Nature though not towards man, that passionate detachment, which *is* the modern attitude to life. The private schools, less at home in the world of industry, technology, and science, gave too much attention to Athens and too little to the atom. Until the 1960s the Common Entrance Examination for public schools still covered Latin! But no science! The classical education received by the hereditary social classes of Britain was part of their undoing. It led them to overvalue the past, Rome and Athens as well as their own history. It induced a fatalistic acceptance of the decline of the British Empire which had to follow the Roman precedent. The meritocracy replaced Gibbon by Galton, and once teachers and ideas interchanged freely, the grammar persuaded the former public schools to adapt themselves more completely to a scientific age. So quickly did some of them learn, that Eton was in fact the first school to install a cyclotron, and Christ's Hospital the first to send a parcel of boys to the moon.

The gain was not all one way. Education for leadership was the professed aim of the public schools; and mighty was their empire until soldiers and administrators succumbed to scientists and technicians. With integration the grammar schools were able to share in that part of the tradition which was still of value and so pursue their vocation of cultivating the élite with all the more confidence. Public schools had learnt how to release children from dependence on their families by creating substitutes for the narrow loyalties of kinship. The grammar schools needed all the more to do the same since so many of their pupils came from homes belonging to a lower culture, and they borrowed some of the same techniques. Eye-witness accounts vouch for the value of the full development of the house system, of the regular dedication meetings in the laboratory and of the week-end and evening clubs for scientific and other hobbies. These have become so active that adolescent children no longer need to spend any of their spare time with their families. Their homes have become simply hotels, to the great benefit of the children.

4. PROGRESS OF INTELLIGENCE TESTING

The success of these reforms depended upon continuous growth in the efficiency of selection methods. How pointless it would have been to set aside superior schools without the means of identifying the elect! Progress did not, of course, always proceed at the same pace on each of these complementary tasks. By and large, the seclusion of grammar schools went ahead more smoothly than selection of pupils. But the more widely recognized it was that better schools should be reserved for the more able, the greater the pressure upon the educational psychologists to improve their techniques. They responded. Necessity once again played its customary part.

Following 1944, there was a large increase in the demand for grammar school places without any corresponding expansion of supply. Competition was sharper; how were the winners to be picked? The value of intelligence tests as a guide to personnel selection in the Forces had been fully demonstrated during the war, and it was therefore natural to adopt the same kind of method for the peace-time purpose, especially in a stratified society prepared by habit of mind to recognize a hierarchy of intelligence as soon as it was pointed out. The results were remarkable: by 1950, merely a few years after the Act, most of the children in the country were taking these tests before they left their primary schools, and, although older methods of examination were also used, high I.Q. was established as the chief qualification for entry to the élite. Educational psychology assumed a central place in pedagogy from which it was never later entirely dislodged.

Progress in the next decades was, it is true, slowed down by socialist obstruction. The people who campaigned for the common school constantly attacked the segregation of clever from stupid which it was the purpose of intelligence tests to accomplish. From their point of view this was quite consistent: once grant their premise that everyone was in some unexplained way the equal of everyone else, and it became as sensible to decry the efficiency of the means by which children were classified one above the other as it was to condemn the consequences. If one child was not in fact more able than another, then intelligence tests *must* be a fraud. The critics mocked the psychologists, and seemed to think their case was proved when they declared (quite rightly) that the tests did not, and could not, measure the abstraction of all-round intelligence. All the critics did was to surround the subject with further verbal confusion. The confusion was to some degree inevitable (as with physics in the seventeenth century) in a new branch of science touching, as it did, upon strong commitments to metaphysics. How could men be equal in the eyes of God and yet unequal in the eyes of the Psychologist?

The socialists made the muddle worse. Very few laymen could at first understand that intelligence was not an abstraction, but an operational concept. Psychologists were not assessing all-round intelligence, there is no such thing, but the qualities needed to benefit from a higher education. If this bundle of qualities was labelled as 'intelligence', that was only done as a convenience. The test of the tests was empirical: did they work? And the answer was that on the whole they did. Most of the children who scored high on the tests also performed well in the grammar schools. It was really a statistical question, a matter of establishing that high performance in the tests (they could have been called the Idiocy tests for all the difference it would have made) was correlated[1] with high performance in the

1. One might add, it was also correlated with performance in other tests for verbal ability, verbal fluency, numerical ability, spatial ability, perceptual ability, memory; for driving ability, accident proneness, digital dexterity, analogizing power, mechanical aptitude, clerical aptitude, emotional maturity; for tone discrimination, sexual attraction, taste sensitivity, colour blindness, accuracy, persistence, neurosis, and powers of observation. Results

grammar school, high performance at the university, and high performance in life. It must be admitted that the psychologists and sociologists were somewhat slow in devising tests for the tests; many of them were still tangled in thickets of ideology. They were not all as clear-sighted as that High Master who urged that 'the greatest encouragement must be given to those researches designed to relate the subsequent success of men and women selected for various purposes with the diagnosis of their capacities given by different methods'.[1] His advice was not fully taken until later.

The socialists were not alone in the wilderness. For a time they succeeded in partially discrediting the I.Q., and, at the height of their influence in the fifties and sixties, frightened a number of local education committees into abandoning the tests altogether. But their success was bound to be short-lived. Every time they were presented with a fresh crop of children, the authorities had to find some way of separating the wheat from the chaff. How? If they discarded intelligence tests, they were thrown back on results of ordinary written examinations, and if they discarded the written examinations, they were thrown back on teachers' reports. They were then in even greater trouble. The teachers had a hard enough job to do in all conscience without forcing them to bear the resentment of every parent whose child they failed. Teachers had to be protected. 'Progressive' authorities were sometimes faced by demands from their own teachers to restore the I.Q. What was more, research demonstrated conclusively that teachers' reports

are nowadays all coded on the one National Intelligence card which accompanies a person throughout his life, unless he has conscientious objections.

1. James, E., op. cit.

and ordinary examinations were less fair to lower-class children. Teachers unconsciously favoured children from their own class; old-fashioned exams were kinder to the more cultured homes. Intelligence tests, less biased, were the very instrument of social justice, a finding which not even the most fanatical socialists of that day could totally ignore.

More moderate socialists, infected with mysticism too, though less virulently, drugged themselves with the belief that the efficiency of selection would remain so low that many able children would always escape the net. They dare not openly espouse inefficient selection and urge that some clever children should be denied opportunity for their faculties; but, privately, they welcomed it – when it happened. They were the secret Catholics in a Protestant town. In the transition period from a pre-merit society, this was a happy adjustment, a source of personal peace of mind, yet no barrier to progress. But it was the comfort of the ostrich. These moderate mystics should have known that you cannot stop the march of science; or rather, since they knew, they should have heeded. Once human behaviour began to be studied systematically, so that once gained, knowledge was cumulative, nothing could arrest the steady advance in techniques for testing and, with the tests, selecting, the bearers of different combinations of genes.

Progress was, as always, uneven, a period of stability being succeeded by a sudden jump forward. Man had to wait until 1989 for the leap of the century. Long before that the 'cyberneticists' had realized that man would best understand his own brain when he could imitate it. As men became more like machines, machines became more like men, and when machines were

73

built to mimic people, the ventriloquist at last understood himself. Modern mental capacity standards date from that year, a common unit of measurement being possible as soon as it was realized that a machine also can have its 'intelligence' tested and scored as much as a human brain. 'Pamela', Bird's pi-computer in the National Physiological Laboratory, with its constant I.Q. of 100, became the recognized national standard, and all the questions in the examination papers were first put to her before being distributed to the schools and other centres.

Well before 1989, psychologists had succeeded in identifying the problems which had to be solved. They realized that the brain was no more separable than the sexual organs from the biochemical economy of the individual, and the individual no more separable than his lungs from the environment, social as well as physical, in which he lived. Many people with high potential intelligence were prevented from making use of it by anxiety due to psychic disturbances. Some had lower intelligence, others higher, when the environment was unfavourable. Hence the I.Q. berserkers with an I.Q. of 140 at some times and 90 at others, and not only when in love or before breakfast – an affliction from which some leading members of the Technicians Party are alleged to suffer. Psychologists tackled the task of bringing the actual nearer to the potential. Advances in therapy were a beneficent by-product of educational selection.

The Spens Committee said in 1938 that it is 'possible at an early age to predict with some degree of accuracy the ultimate level of a child's intellectual powers'. That is true now; it was not true then. No wonder resentment was aroused when the main tests were given once, at eleven! A person's performance at that one age decided whether he went to a grammar school. If he failed he could, in theory, get a second chance later on. In practice he seldom did. Late developers were too late. The boy or girl whose capacity flowered even as young as fourteen was lucky indeed to get a transfer from a modern to a grammar school. He was usually stuck with the stupid, and classed with them for the rest of his life. That was a cruel injustice for the individual and a shocking waste for society – so much so that in a small way comprehensive schools actually did some good by making it easier for people to swim from one stream to another. People knew that in some people intelligence reached its height at twelve, in others it only came to full fruition at thirty – but they did not act as if they knew. As this truth was driven home, educators sought, with increasing success, to make intelligence assessment continuous throughout school life. I.Q.s were tested at seven, nine, eleven, thirteen, and fifteen, and at each stage a person whose score was higher than it had been previously was taken away from his inferiors and lodged with his equals. Yet the people whose ability developed only when they had left school escaped the net of selection altogether. Even in the 1980s, a man who suddenly came to his senses at the age of twenty-five had the greatest difficulty in securing proper recognition for his talents.

Here it is that the modern development of adult education has proved so vital. School came to last for life. By the end of the century the right of every person to be judged according to his ability was honoured in more than the breach. It was at last accepted that, as a matter of quite elementary justice, neither man nor child should be judged stupid until he was proved to be. The presumption was always of cleverness. So at *any* age *any* person became entitled, more than entitled, encouraged to apply every five years for re-test at a Regional Centre for Adult Education, and if his hopes were realized, then justice was invariably done. The copy of his National Intelligence card at H.Q. was destroyed, and a new card substituted containing the re-test score, so that no employer (or fiancée) who applied in the ordinary way for his I.Q. and aptitude scores would ever know about the lowlier status he had once had. It was also decided in the Courts that there was no obligation on anyone to put anything more than his current I.Q. in his *Who's Who* entry. A successful re-test was quite genuinely a fresh start.

No doubt this has led to difficulties. Some children have become excessively ambitious on behalf of their parents and have exerted too much pressure on them to strive for reclassification. Books on the care of parents have become too avidly studied. Some workmen have displayed jealousy when their elderly workmates have been sent away to university or gymnasium. But in the long interim period while methods of selection have been in process of improvement, the disadvantages have been far outweighed by the advantages. Now, of course, the psychologists have refined their methods to such a point that they can allow for most of the imponderables which delay development and forecast not only the I.Q. but the ages at which it will fructify. Exciting as the advance is to every scientifically-minded person, it has to be admitted that the discussions it has unloosed have been grist to the critics of the established order.

5. SUMMARY

This chapter has sketched once again the great story of educational reform. The government, when won round to a contemporary sense of values, recognized that no spending was more productive than spending on the generation of brain-power. Miserliness became munificence, teachers and school buildings a first charge upon the national income. The independence of the grammar schools was preserved. The better public schools were merged and cross-fertilized with the grammar schools. The new system was sustained by methods of identifying ability that became steadily more effective. By the 1980s the foundations of our modern system of education had been laid.

Progress was possible because, as I explained in a previous chapter, the socialists collapsed as an organized force. The same thing did not happen to the sentiments they expressed. All babies are creeping socialists and some never grow out of it. But the hard core of psychological egalitarians who never recover from the envies of the nursery only become a danger to the State when they are joined by large numbers of other people whose hopes are thwarted in adult life. The 1960s were one of those times, the present day another. People were frustrated then because they (or their children) were deprived of the superior education to which they imagined themselves entitled; people are frustrated now for the same reason, not so much by segregation in the schools (most people have got used to that now) as by the suggestion that the Regional Centres for Adult Education have outlived their usefulness. The Centres have become much prized by some of the more capable technicians, the very kind of people who, though lowly, are just intelligent enough to have been the core of every revolutionary movement. Is not any hint of closing the doors of the regional centres bound to arouse discontent? If my analysis is correct, this new departure, as I shall explain more fully later on, is one of the underlying reasons for the recent troubles.

CHAPTER FOUR

FROM SENIORITY TO MERIT

1. THE CLASS OF OLD MEN

FOR a half-century schools were the target for reform, and quite rightly too, the achievement was brilliant. But the reformers were as always (perhaps had to be) too single-minded. They focused on schools to the exclusion of everything else, with the distressing result that for many years the efficiency with which manpower was used in industry lagged far behind the efficiency with which it was used in education. Our grandfathers did not fully realize that promotion of adults by merit, with all that it implied for industrial organization, was as necessary as promotion of children by merit. A society which acknowledged the claims of talent in the schools, but not in industry, was a house divided against itself. They did not fully understand that when castes were abolished, or rather converted into our modern kind of classes, there was still another category of people to circumvent – the class of old men. They did not fully appreciate that having the wrong man in a position of power merely because he was of superior age was every bit as wasteful as having the wrong man in a position of power merely because his parents were of a superior class. In an open society the few who are chosen out of the many who are called should be chosen on merit; age is as much an irrelevant criterion as birth.

Within the span of human history age has been the most enduring ruling class: once established, every aristocracy, every plutocracy, every bureaucracy, has also been a gerontocracy; and even under democracy, government by the people, of the people, for the people, meant government by old people, of young people, for old people. In pre-industrial times the autocrat of the farm did not share his authority with any schoolmaster when his sons were young, and he retained his dominion over them when they were grown men, restrained only by the fear that if he irked his children overmuch his eventual fate might be that of King Lear. After the introduction of industry, fathers still did all they could to secure advancement for their own over other men's sons, but never over themselves, and to this end the solidarity of seniority made all fathers into a band of brothers. After the establishment of the new élite fathers could no longer gain privilege for their own sons, but they still continued to do all they could to ensure that other men's sons, however able, did not gain supremacy over themselves.

The meritocracy threatened, in short, to become yet another gerontocracy. Had this danger not been averted, the intellectual revolution would have been incomplete.

With education reformed, some people imagined they had matriculated to the millennium. The winners from school and university were inclined to lean upon their laurels. They entered, as if to a haven, professions still governed by a restrictive guild mentality. They accepted rule by the elders of their profession. They comforted themselves that they would continue to make the same steady progression through the age-grades as they had done at school, until in proper season they became sacred elders in their turn. It was only the relentless facts of the modern world which roused people from their torpor and sent competition to storm industry as well as school. In order to combine the best of England, our régime for children, with the best of America, their régime for adults, competition had to last for life.

2. FACTORIES CEASE TO BE SCHOOLS

Up till the Hitler war and for some years after, education determined prospects for promotion almost as much as it does in modern times. The manual worker who left school at the minimum age ordinarily remained a manual worker for life, the farthest he could go being to charge-hand and foreman, or, if he was lucky, by another route to general secretary of a trade union. The progress chaser taken away early from grammar school might climb to works manager, the pay-clerk to accountant. In most work-places it was practically impossible to transfer from the ladder selected to start with according to the age at which the boy left school to another ladder which would take him higher; the foreman remained a foreman instead of beginning again on the ladder of works management, the accountant remained an accountant and was not in the running for director. Education decided the point of entry to industry, and the point of entry decided where one finished up.

This structure would have been well enough had the schools been rationalized. But when neither quality nor quantity of education were yet determined by intelligence, many clever children left school too soon, many stupid too late. A minority of more perceptive employers, following the civil service model which I have already described, set out to correct the injustices of the educational system and profit themselves at the same time. They gave their clever employees opportunities to rise within the firm in place of the opportunities they had missed at school. At its most complete (and to us most ridiculous), this practice made it possible for the tea-boy from the manual workers and the office-boy from the clerical to rise up to the board of directors. The first industries to be nationalized made some effort to do at least as well as the civil service. On British Railways a clerk could, for instance, if he moved off the lowest rungs when he was very young, transfer from the clerical ladder to one of the lower administrative posts.[1] Electricity supply was more enlightened still.

Employees in the industry are considered to be on a common ladder, rising as openings occur, and in open competition according to experience and ability for the particular vacancy.[2]

The statement is entertaining, practice not being quite like precept, because it shows how it was thought things should work. Some employers were so proud of their promotion schemes and ladder plans that they preferred to take on children straight from school and train them on the job than recruit university graduates. This attitude was regrettably common amongst leading executives who had not been to university themselves; there were of course many such 'self-made men' in those distant days. The school's shame was the factory's pride.

The beginning of the second phase, which has lasted until the present day, is usually put in the 1950s. The 1944 Act took ten to twenty years before its effect was generally felt in industry. Not many employers were as quick as the High Master to see its significance.

1. For an account see Acton Society Trust. *Training and Promotion in Nationalized Industry.* 1950.

2. *Report of a Committee of Enquiry into the Electricity Supply Industry.* Para. 171. Cmd. 9672, 1956.

No longer, said Sir Eric, *will industry or commerce be able to recruit at fifteen or sixteen boys who, as in the past, are of a quality to work their way up to positions of the highest managerial responsibility.*[1]

In the fullness of time only the most dim-witted employers failed to learn this lesson. The evidence came through the door at the end of every term. Whatever opportunities there might be for secondary modern children to climb the industrial ladder, the hard fact was that fewer and fewer of them had the ability to do so. The grammar schools were retaining the 'likely lads' who in previous generations might have entered industry as fifteen-year-olds, and the cleverest of the clever were going on to the university. Since the only ladder plan that mattered was the educational one, the captains of industry had to fit in with that. Either they could attract a share of grammar school graduates, and a seasoning from the university; or their businesses would perish. To sustain top management they had to recruit cadets from higher education, even if it meant incurring the hostility of the trade unions to introducing outsiders, particularly well-educated outsiders. The union leaders claimed, in the interests of their own members, that a man who had 'come up the hard way' by working his passage upwards was inherently superior to others of purely academic education. But that was before education came to be held in the high respect it later enjoyed. The view was obvious nonsense – there was no harder way of coming up than the grammar school.

Awareness that shortage of talent was more serious than any other fanned the competition between business

1. James, E., op. cit.

executives. According to a contemporary report only a few years after 1944 –

One young man in his second year at university had already been offered a post at £750 by one large company for when he should graduate, and was being assiduously courted by another vast company, whose managing director entertained him to lunch.[1]

This was nothing to what happened later; eventually every forward-looking company had its teams of talent scouts combing the universities and grammar schools and most science masters and lecturers were offered retainers if they would regularly supply reports on promising students. Newspapers were filled with employers' appeals to scholars; college magazines grew larger and larger on the proceeds of advertisements. This hectic competition was sometimes unfair, as many trade associations alleged, and sometimes led to abuse. Some clever grammar school pupils were dissuaded from continuing into the sixth forms by offers of generous apprenticeships, and others from seeking admission to the university by glib scouts who promised them not only high salaries immediately but university education later at company expense. Retainers and assistance with research expenses were not the best way of augmenting science teachers' salaries.

The N.U.S. (National Union of Students) and B.U.G.S.A. had to protect their members and in 1969 the Ministry of Education and the Federation of British Industries drew up the Code of Fair Practice for Utilizing the Products of Higher Education. Although a worthy endeavour, this proved so ineffective in practice that government control over the allocation of intellectual resources became imperative. When it was

1. Acton Society Trust, op. cit.

instituted priorities could be generally enforced. Effective brain-power planning is not only necessary to end one of the kinds of competition between employers that is wasteful, but gives the government strategic power to control the whole economy.

3. CHALLENGE TO AGE

Industry surrendered to teachers the function of selecting recruits for management with a good enough grace when it saw that surrender was essential to survival. From that time on most of those who at the ages of nineteen or twenty-three entered the higher reaches of industry, commerce, and the professions were the pick of their age-groups. Managerial cadets were chosen on merit through competitive selection in the schools. But there, in this transition period, free competition stopped. As soon as the newcomer arrived in factory or office, he no longer had the chance to pit his talents against all and sundry in the promotion stakes. He was no longer permitted, even after he had spent several years learning the business, to stand up in open competition with people much older than himself. While he was a *junior* man, whether he had the capacity of Henry Ford or Lord Nuffield it made no matter, he had to be content with being at best a *junior* executive. In all the most important jobs promotion was still by seniority, so much so that without exceptional luck even the best-educated could not hope to reach the top of the ladder until they were fifty or sixty. The story of the third and most recent phase is the story of the way in which the principle of seniority has gradually yielded to the principle of merit, and industry been modelled on the schools.

It is once again difficult for us to realize how strongly

entrenched the old were in those days, especially in Britain. Status for age had once been linked with hereditary status, but it was far less easy to discredit. By the middle of last century it was extremely rare to hear anyone openly defending a hereditary system. Kinship connexions were no longer thought to confer merit on a man. But age was. The rights of the old did not have to be publicly acclaimed, they were so widely taken for granted. Age was accorded deference for no better reason than that, and people did not even have to acknowledge the existence of any dilemma when on the one hand they talked in favour of promotion by merit and on the other acted in favour of promotion by age. They resolved the dilemma before it was properly posed by enormously over-estimating the value of 'experience' which was imagined to be the product purely of years. There was a mystique about it: people said 'Ah, yes, but he's got more experience', as though that was the last word. Respect for age was as much the rule of society as respect for the aristocracy from which it had grown.

Seniores priores – there is no stronger testament to its influence than the schools. They weakened their own progressive role by upholding the very principle with which they were fundamentally at loggerheads. Prefects were one of the most distinctive features of the old public schools. These prefects were older boys who exercised day-to-day government over their younger fellows, some of whom were selected as 'fags' to perform the duties of servants. The maintenance of discipline was in large part the responsibility of the prefects, who had the power to secure obedience by beating any little boy who incurred their displeasure. The prefect system was unfortunately taken over by the grammar schools too.

Consequently, the regard younger children always have for older was converted into an awe which often lasted for life. The old, by allowing the young to have authority when it was not a threat to themselves, helped to ensure that their own power would later go unchallenged. The abolition of prefects was an important reform which started in the 'progressive' co-educational schools and later spread to the more orthodox.

I have no space to trace the subtle and individually infinitesimal changes which have combined to create a new spirit; all I can do is to pinpoint some of the counter-forces which have in the end proved too strong for the gerontocracy. I will deal briefly with each of them in turn.

1. *Pressure from the young.* No solid progress could be made until the young had generated more confidence in themselves. As long as they accepted the dominance of the old there was no hope of a shift in the distribution of power, any more than there had been any hope of change while the superiority of the higher classes in a hereditary system was recognized by the lower. The right of the old to power had first to be questioned as strenuously as the legitimacy of inheritance, and for the same reason. Inheritance was denounced for the simple reason that a developing industrial country in competition with others could no longer afford second-rate leaders; the needs of the economy reshaped society. This campaign was not called off just because one victory had been won, but was turned against the old. Members of every fresh generation revolted against their elders; youth of mettle to oppose the pretensions of age instead of siding with it for the sake of favours to come. Some cried destruction on the established order, some

tried, more constructively, to remove the blocks to their own advancement. The most rebellious knew instinctively that the fastest progress occurs anywhere when the old have to surrender their power before their span of life is complete – the essence of every social revolution is the earlier transfer of authority from one generation to another; the wisest knew that the surest progress is made by the mouse, by nibbling at the establishment instead of by taking arms against it. The best policy was to criticize the worth of individual old people in an empirical manner rather than the class as a whole.

The young succeeded as much as they did in opposing private practice because they had the resources of the public culture to support them. They declared that youth was generally entitled, on the grounds of merit, to more preferment than it received. They were quite right. In any rapidly changing society the young are more at home than the old: it is easier for them to learn for the first time than for the old to unlearn, and learn again, for a second or third time, especially when nostalgia for their own youth makes the old disinclined even to try. This is more than ever true when the schools are progressing even more rapidly than their host society. Then children not only learn different things, attuned to the needs of their own day (particularly when the teachers are also young); they also learn more because standards are higher and methods of pedagogy better. Compare the boy who learns physics today with an elderly man who was at the same university in the eighties before Shag was even born. The change is so dramatic, it is not really the same subject at all. Given the same native ability, there is no doubt which of them should obtain an important post in the laboratories, say at H.Q. in Eugenics House. I say 'given the same native ability' – but of course this is implausible. The content of higher education has not only advanced; methods of selecting those to benefit from it have improved at least as fast. Each ten-year age-cohort of the élite has up till recently had more innate capacity than the previous one; the university alumnus of 2000 more talent, as well as better training, than the alumnus of 1990; of 2010 more than of 2000. The revelation that the graduate of 2020 was only very slightly superior to the graduate of 2010 is one of the disturbing facts which has led to the present turmoil.

2. *Support from the old.* There was never any hard-and-fast division between young and old: class-lines were always blurred. Some easy-going young people welcomed age-stratification for the sake of a quiet life, without spur to compete with their peers. Some old people were, on the other hand, 'traitors to their age-group'. Observance of promotion by seniority, though it was in the interests of most older people, was never in the interests of all of them.

Nearly every non-manual occupation was age-graded. A bank clerk, for instance, started at the bottom and then every few years added an increment to his salary and a notch to his status, until eventually he became chief cashier or even branch manager. But if he lost his job, say at the age of forty, it might be through no fault of his own, perhaps as a result of office-automation,[1] what was he to do then? After Labour's first

1. The large firm, with a wide spread of interests, could offer greater security, which was one of its attractions for many young people, and one of the causes of the relative growth of the large-scale units in the economy.

National Superannuation Act he could at least take his pension with him. But not his status. If he tried to enter another bank, or another employment altogether, on to what rung of the promotion ladder was he to step? If he started at the beginning again, he would suffer the loss of all the increments he had received in twenty years. If at the same level as other men of forty, he would be filling a position coveted by an existing employee of thirty-five. This was usually ruled out by the opposition of all the younger people in the line of promotion. Since the old insisted on preferment for seniority, to protect themselves, they could not turn about when the same principle was invoked by the young, on behalf of their own prospects of slow but steady ascent. Consequently the old were only secure as long as they remained in one employment – middle-aged fear of dismissal was a main cause of the caution which led to stagnation in many companies. They were terrified by the cry of 'too old at forty', a maxim feared by all except the outstandingly brilliant whom no age-barrier could halt.

The middle-aged, who had to accept demotion to get any job at all after they had once lost their place on the ladder, were sometimes as keen on promotion by merit as the younger colleagues whose inferior status they shared. That was a useful alliance for youth. Another, stronger one was struck up with the retired. Early and fixed retirement from work was the consequence of promotion by seniority. The usual retirement age was at one time sixty-five. However able the manager, and however anxious he was to continue, he was under great pressure not to. If he postponed his retirement by a couple of years, the whole shuffling progress below him came to a stop. The assistant manager of sixty had to wait two extra years for his promotion, so did the deputy assistant manager of fifty-five, so did the assistant deputy assistant manager of fifty, all the way down to the lad of thirty just recently post-graduated from the university. They were all waiting for the 'old man' to start pottering in his garden instead of with the business, hoping that they would not become too exhausted waiting for his desk. Every age-grade therefore united against the top to ensure that the rules of the game were kept. Before the meritocracy was fully established, age-stratification as a substitute for the hereditary order may have been necessary for the sake of social stability. But the cost was very high. Every year hundreds of thousands of elderly men, some of whom would have been much more assets than liabilities to their employers, were forced to retreat into idleness, and deprived of their own self-esteem, by the rigidity of the promotion system. Those who thought they would have held on to their posts on grounds of ability alone naturally sided with the youngsters who expected they would achieve more rapid promotion if the rules were changed.

The consequences of disregarding merit became more and more serious with the increasing number of old people who lasted out their span of life, and the lengthening of that span. The elderly were not merely the only large reserve of labour and intelligence, they were also a growing one. Eventually Britain was constrained to follow the example of other industrial societies with less out-of-date retirement rules. But when the retiring age was raised to seventy, the political consequences were so grave that we had to wait twenty years for the age to be raised further to eighty, and another twelve years before the fixed age was abolished altogether. Raising the age quickened the spread of the new principles, for seniority lost its appeal when all the people waiting in the promotion queue suddenly had their prospects darkened; they became more willing to put their trust in merit. The elderly whose retirement had been postponed did not usually stay as leaders; few people over fifty-five are today in full membership of the meritocracy. They had (like manual workers before them) to reconcile themselves to demotion as their capacity fell off, measured either absolutely or relatively to new arrivals from the schools. The managing director had to become an office mechanic in someone else's firm if not in his own; the professor an assistant in the library. There have been judges who have become taxi-drivers, bishops curates, and publishers writers – the old shine in jobs where reliability is important. The re-employment of retired people performed one great service by dissociating authority from age. Youngsters used to feel uncomfortable when giving orders to old people otherwise in the same social class as themselves. The re-employed showed so little resentment towards their youthful superiors, they were so thankful to have work at all, that the diffidence of their youthful superiors was dispelled, and their confidence in command more nearly equated to their abilities.

3. *Improvement of merit-rating.* Perhaps the greatest reason for the change in mental climate is that merit has become progressively more measurable. In the old days seniority had the splendid advantage of being an objective standard, even if it was irrelevant, whereas merit was still subjective even though relevant. Indeed, for a long time, 'merit' was little more than a respectable disguise for nepotism. Fathers secured promotion for their relatives and friends, and pretended to themselves and to others they were doing nothing except give merit

its due. But if they concealed their fault from themselves, others were not so easily deceived. The trade unions, in particular, were only too well aware of the pitfalls of selecting by 'merit', when the father was his own judge and psychologist, and were justifiably suspicious that when outsiders were introduced into the line of promotion something less than justice had been done. They therefore stood by promotion by seniority, which was at least one better than vile nepotism. The world could see whether, according to this particular idea of fairness, right prevailed or not. If on any ladder, a man of thirty was given superiority over a man of forty (or rather a man with ten years' service preferred to a man with twenty), then all could see the miscarriage of justice.

This vicious circle – the vagueness of merit leading to its rejection – was only broken when the means of selection employed in the schools were adapted for use in the economy. Intelligence tests and aptitude tests were objective, and a good deal more reliable than the older forms of examination which they supplemented. The first stage, as we have seen, was for the level of performance achieved in the tests (when taken together with the level of education with which the test results were correlated) to determine the level of entry into industry. Once people were ready, it was then but a step to extend the sway of the tests until the markings controlled promotion as well as selection. To begin with, employers had to submit candidates to their own house-tests; yet such was the suspicion in industrial relations at that time, their impartiality was distrusted just because they were the employer's responsibility. The atmosphere was much sweetened when the government established its chain of Regional Adult Education Centres and community centres as a common service to industry, and, after a very long and acrimonious debate, gave employers access to the results of intelligence tests from the Centres as well as the schools. Employers now have as close an interest as employees in the quinquennial re-valuations at the regional centres, and many of them show their appreciation on the Prize Days of their factories.

One thing the regional centres could not do. They could not measure the qualities of character expressed in effort expended by an employee in the course of his work. Intelligence and effort together make up merit $(I + E = M)$. The lazy genius is not one. Here employers have made their own contribution to the cause of progress. 'Scientific management' pioneered by Taylor, the Galbraiths, and Bedaux has led to modern time and motion study, and this in its turn to the measurement of effort. The art of work measurement has become more of a science, with the consequence that wages can be assessed, and related to effort, in a more and more precise manner. I shall return to this subject in a later chapter. Dr Roskill's great contribution was to show how the principle of work study could be applied to mental processes. After that the employer had by him a Roskill chart as well as the scores from the education centres, and if he chose wrongly withal, it was high time he had a re-test himself. The trade unions' right of access to management scores is one of the guarantees that, if new tests are necessary, they will be administered willy-nilly.

4. SUMMARY

These, then, are some of the steps by which the old rigidities have been removed from industry. When intelligent public opinion as a whole recognized that efficiency *must* be raised, in the general interest of mankind as well as of the part of it inhabiting these islands, the claims of youth could not be denied. Emergency was youth's opportunity. This was shown in every war – the young denounced 'brass-hats' and 'politicians' because they were out of date, and made headway precisely because bad brass-hats and bad politicians would have let the enemy in at the gates. International competition was also effective in peace. Native ability frozen in inferior age-groups or inferior social classes always had one strong ally – the clever foreigner.

Change has, as always too, created its own resistance. The protests of the past were the protests of youth. By rebelling against conventions and restrictions imposed on them by their elders, they at last made a new world. Where youth is the leader, age is the led; and not all old people have submitted to their new inferiority. Every now and then an old man, overtaken by a younger, and disappointed in work, turns to blame not so much his successor as the social order which makes possible the indignity he feels. He may not play rebel as grandly as the young man a hundred years ago – the outlandish narrow trousers, draped coats, and beards which some old men sport are a trifle pathetic – but he has the same kind of discontent, springing from the same sources. We do not need to look further for one of the strands in the support given to the reformers. In the light of sociology the old men at their meetings do not seem so much at odds with the vivid young girls on the platform.

*

I have now finished the first part of my essay, and with it my sketch of the means by which opportunities were equalized. Since I have had to compress more than a century's progress into a few pages, I am aware that I have done less than justice to the part of individuals in the intellectual renaissance. Too severe a sociological analysis may suggest that history has slid to its present conclusion as inevitably as the morning rocket arrives on the moon. That would be quite wrong. There is nothing mechanical about history. Stupidity has not been routed by sociology, but by the heroes who have combined high conscience with high intelligence. Think of Sidney and Beatrice Webb, and Bernard Shaw – the modern Conservative Party is carrying on their battle; think of Forster, Fisher, Ramsay MacDonald, Butler, Wyatt, Crosland, Stewart, Hailsham, Taylor, Dobson, and Clauson – their cause was our cause. What the Populists have done by their recent apostasy is to forfeit any right to claim descent from these great men and women. The Technicians have surrendered the mantle of greatness to the Conservatives.

The great political theorists of the past century changed the mental climate of their time by reinterpreting old values in terms of new situations – for instance, by hailing the post-1944 educational system in the name of equality. They appealed in a characteristically empirical manner to the common-sense predicament of our island in a common-sense, competitive world. Supporting the theorists were the great administrators. They called out the psychologists and protected them from public assault. They made the grammar schools the élite's training ground. They battered the Treasury into accepting the new view of economy – that to spend money on education was in the long run the only way of raising the national product, and with it, the taxable capacity of the country. They overcame by a hundred expedients the unsavoury obscurantism of the public schools, and eventually promoted their amalgamation with the other kind of grammar school. They dethroned the old and made youth the prince of industry. Let us praise them all.

*

But I have written this essay less to honour famous men than to warn my fellow intelligences. I said so at the beginning of this book, and I say again, that we shall show ourselves unworthy of our scholarships if we scorn our opponents. As individuals, I agree, few are exceptional. But as a mass they are formidable, the more so because by its forward motion the society *we* have created renews *their* strength daily. I shall be more explicit. Who are the lower classes of modern England? We can distinguish two main groups:

(1) The majority who are second-generation lower class. These comprise all the offspring of lower-class parents except for clever children who have risen higher by means of the educational ladder.
(2) The minority who are first-generation lower class. These are the stupid offspring of upper-class parents, found out in the schools and demoted to the social class appropriate to their inferior capacity.

I shall return to the first group, numerically overwhelming, in Part Two of this book, for I want to attempt there the difficult task of showing, against the background of their general status in society, why we can expect even some of these native proletarians to be

D   97

discontented. For the moment, in order to make my point as forcefully as I can, I shall do no more than discharge the easier task of drawing attention to the resentment in the second group, the stupid born of the clever.

Painstaking retrospective study (for which the University of York has earned a well-deserved reputation) has made it seem at least reasonably probable that before the 1980s 'downward mobility' was uncommon. Upper-class parents with dull children did everything possible to hide their handicap. They usually made up by their own frantic determination for any lack of will on the part of their children. For instance, they bought places at private schools which would never have been awarded on merit. They spent, for the sake of stimulus, even more on books and travel than other rich people. And, when the combined pressure of home and school had produced, as it often did, a person superficially not too dull, the parents eased the loved one into a cosy corner of one of the less exacting professions, such as law or stockbroking. These anti-social parents were able to keep a hold on the old professions and also on family firms which for one reason or another enjoyed some small but effective monopoly. The old upper class found jobs for nearly *all* its children, while most of the additional jobs in the new professions, especially in science and technology, went to cadets drawn from the lower classes. The old upper class in absolute terms suffered but little diminution, merely lost its relative predominance at a time when the proportion of white-collar jobs in the economy was increasing fast.

After the 1980s the scene began to change very rapidly. I suppose the decisive innovation was the recognition of merit in industry, and at last even in the professions. The stupid found it harder and harder to pass as clever. They found it harder and harder to get through the selection boards, and if they managed to squeeze through, their incapacity for work becoming more and more demanding was as often as not spotted by increasingly efficient personnel departments. After the reform of the public schools they were also deprived of the chance of a first-class education, unless it was procured at truly colossal expense by hiring private tutors. Nitwits could still go to second-rate public schools – can even do so today if their parents are wealthy enough – but what was the use, if the education was second-rate?

The closing of the bolt-holes has been made less irksome by the fine work of the Regional Centres in one of their less well-known manifestations. The Commissioners have persuaded many parents that, if they love their stupid children, they will not cloud their lives with a lie – by pretending to them and everyone else that an I.Q. of 90 is really one of 110. I do not for one moment contend that modern notions of parental duty are everywhere accepted, but I would still maintain that we need not be too anxious about the older generation. There are so few clever parents with nothing but stupid progeny, with a whole brood of ugly ducklings. The younger generation have reacted less well, I mean the children who can fool themselves no longer after they have suffered dismal results in successive examinations. They are brought up in our most honoured homes, and, as infants, share the esteem which the community accords to their fathers and mothers. They may, too, get used to a standard of life which they will never again enjoy once they have entered a manual occupation at the appropriate level. Reared in a house with an entertainment centre at its core, bespoke cooking and open wood fires, the poor boy may find it hard indeed to get used to an ordinary council house with heat pump but no open fires, with three-dimensional tape-recorders instead of an entertainment centre, with pre-packaged meals instead of bespoke cooking. The rest of his life may be a backward look; scientific selection for jobs, though it has done much, has not taken all the moodiness out of nostalgia. Of course it may not happen like this. To be truthful, we cannot yet be sure just how much resentment the *déclassé* person does feel. The very fact that he is stupid means that he is inarticulate, and the fact that he is inarticulate means that he cannot explain too clearly how he does feel. Some psychologists who have specialized on these subjects have advanced the theory, which I myself find perfectly plausible, that they do suffer, but have been prevented by their intellectual limitations from saying so. Certainly they have not organized any concerted attack on the society of which they might claim to be the victims. Is it not possible that for fifty years some of them have been smouldering for the leadership which they cannot provide for themselves?

PART TWO

DECLINE OF THE
LOWER CLASSES

CHAPTER FIVE

STATUS OF THE WORKER

1. GOLDEN AGE OF EQUALITY

I HAVE in the first part of this book reviewed the means by which our modern élite has been established, and what a splendid result it is! No longer is it just the brilliant individual who shines forth; the world beholds for the first time the spectacle of a brilliant class, the five per cent of the nation who know what five per cent means. Every member is a tried specialist in his own sphere. Mounting at a faster and faster rate, our knowledge has been cumulative from generation to generation. In the course of a mere hundred years we have come close to realizing at one stroke the ideal of Plato, Erasmus, and Shaw. But, if sociology teaches anything, it teaches that no society is completely stable; always there are strains and conflicts. In the first part of this essay I have mentioned some of the tensions – between family and community, between different parts of the educational structure, between young and old, between the *déclassé* and the other members of the proletariat – incident to the rise of the meritocracy. Now I turn, in this second part, to consider from the same point of view, the consequences of progress for the lower class, and, as I have said, particularly for those born into it.

My method of analysis is historical; the comparison I draw once more with a century ago. Taylor has called that time the golden age of equality.[1] A sort of egali-

1. Taylor, F. G. *The Role of Egalitarianism in Twentieth-century England.* 2004.

tarianism flourished then because two contradictory principles for legitimizing power were struggling for mastery – the principle of kinship and the principle of merit – and nearly everyone, in his heart of hearts, believed in both. Everyone thought it proper to advance his son and honour his father; everyone thought it proper to seek out ability and honour achievement. Individuals were riven as much as society. The consequence was that anyone who had reached privilege behind the shield of only one of these principles could be attacked with the sword of the other – the man born great was criticized because, by another reckoning, he did not deserve his fortune; and the base-born achieving greatness could be charged half impostor. The powerful were, by this whirligig, unfailingly unseated.

Many people were catapulted forward by their parents' riches and influence; not only did they benefit from the culture festooning their homes, they were sent to the best schools and colleges, dispatched on trips abroad and given expensive training for Bar, counting-house, or surgery – all the advantages, in short, which we in our day try to keep for the deserving. But since such treatment was sanctioned by only half the moral code, the beneficiaries were only half at home in their station in life. They could not say to themselves with complete conviction 'I am the best man for the job' because they knew that they had not won their place in open competition and, if they were honest, had to recognize that a dozen of their subordinates would have been as good, or perhaps better. Although they sometimes sought to deny self-doubt by too brassy an assertion of self-confidence, such denial was hard to sustain when it plainly ran against the facts. The upper-class man had to be insensitive indeed not to have noticed, at some time in his life, that a private in his regiment, a butler or 'charlady' in his home, a driver of taxi or bus, or the humble workman with lined face and sharp eyes in the railway carriage or country pub – not to have noticed that amongst such people was intelligence, wit, and wisdom at least equal to his own, not to have noticed that every village had its Jude the Obscure. If he had so observed, if he had so recognized that his social inferiors were sometimes his biological superiors, if the great variety of people in all social classes had made him think in some dim way that 'a man's a man for a' that', was he not likely to respond by treating them with a kind of respect?[1]

Even if the superiors deceived themselves, they could not their subordinates. These knew that many bosses were there not so much because of what they knew, as who they knew, and who their parents were, and went on, with wanton exaggeration, to denounce all bosses on like account. Some men of talent took pains (if contemporary novels are to be relied on) to make it known in the factory, if not in the golf club, that they had 'come up the hard way'. But who could tell for certain how far success had been accident, or lack of scruples offset lack of brains? The workmen had their doubts. They let fly with their criticism of the powers-that-be, and so kept even the able under restraint. The energy wasted on criticism and counter-criticism was colossal.

1. In an earlier age the sumptuary laws passed by Henry VII to force lords to eat in the same great hall as their retainers were not only for the benefit of the retainers. In modern times there is nothing to be gained from social mixing, in school, in residence, or at work, because the upper class now have little or nothing to learn from the lower.

An even more important consequence of the conflict in values was that the workers could altogether dissociate their own judgements of themselves from the judgement of society. Subjective and objective status were often poles apart. The worker said to himself: 'Here I am, a workman. Why am I a workman? Am I fit for nothing else? Of course not. Had I had a proper chance I would have shown the world. A doctor? A brewer? A minister? I could have done anything. I never had the chance. And so I am a worker. But don't think that at bottom I am any worse than anyone else. I'm better.' Educational injustice enabled people to preserve their illusions, inequality of opportunity fostered the myth of human equality. Myth we know it to be; not so our ancestors.

2. GULF BETWEEN THE CLASSES

This evocation of the past shows how great the change has been. In those days no class was homogeneous in brains: clever members of the upper classes had as much in common with clever members of the lower classes as they did with stupid members of their own. Now that people are classified by ability, the gap between the classes has inevitably become wider. The upper classes are, on the one hand, no longer weakened by self-doubt and self-criticism. Today the eminent know that success is just reward for their own capacity, for their own efforts, and for their own undeniable achievement. They deserve to belong to a superior class. They know, too, that not only are they of higher calibre to start with, but that a first-class education has been built upon their native gifts. As a result, they can come as close as anyone to understanding the full and ever-growing complexity of our technical civilization. They

are trained in science, and it is scientists who have inherited the earth. What can they have in common with
people whose education stopped at sixteen or seventeen,
leaving them with the merest smattering of dog-science?
How can they carry on a two-sided conversation with
the lower classes when they speak another, richer, and
more exact language? Today, the élite know that, except for a grave error in administration, which should
at once be corrected if brought to light, their social
inferiors are inferiors in other ways as well – that is, in
the two vital qualities, of intelligence and education,
which are given pride of place in the more consistent
value system of the twenty-first century. Hence one of
our characteristic modern problems: some members
of the meritocracy, as most moderate reformers admit,
have become so impressed with their own importance
as to lose sympathy with the people whom they govern,
and so tactless that even people of low calibre have been
quite unnecessarily offended. The schools and universities are endeavouring to instil a more proper sense of
humility – what does even modern man count beside
the wonders which Nature has wrought in the universe?
– but for the moment the efficiency of public relations
with the lower classes is not all that it might be.

As for the lower classes, their situation is different
too. Today all persons, however humble, know they
have had every chance. They are tested again and
again. If on one occasion they are off-colour, they have
a second, a third, and fourth opportunity to demon-
strate their ability. But if they have been labelled
'dunce' repeatedly they cannot any longer pretend;
their image of themselves is more nearly a true, un-
flattering, reflection. Are they not bound to recognize
that they have an inferior status – not as in the past because

they were denied opportunity; but because they *are* inferior?[1] For the first time in human history the inferior man has no ready buttress for his self-regard. This has presented contemporary psychology with its gravest problem. Men who have lost their self-respect are liable to lose their inner vitality (especially if they are inferior to their own parents and fall correspondingly in the social scale) and may only too easily cease to be either good citizens or good technicians. The common man is liable to sulk for his fig-leaf.

The consequences of so depressing the status of the inferior and elevating that of the superior have naturally engaged the full attention of social science. We cannot pretend that its path has always been smooth. Dr Jason's 'tadpole' argument which amounted, when stripped of verbiage, to saying that on the whole all tadpoles were happier because they knew that some of them would turn into frogs, was at best a half-truth. The young might be happier; but what of the many older tadpoles who knew they would never become frogs? The tadpoles only confused counsel. Since Lord Jason himself became a 'frog', research has proceeded more steadily.

The situation has been saved by five things. First, by the philosophy underlying teaching in secondary modern schools. When these were started, no one quite knew what to do about the content of education for the lower classes. Children were taught the three R's as well as how to use simple tools and to measure with

1. This is not entirely a new realization. My colleague, Mr Fallon, has drawn my attention to an old cartoon in the *New Yorker*, an ostensibly humorous American periodical, *circa* 1954. It showed a large psychiatrist confronting a small patient, saying: 'You haven't got an inferiority complex. You *are* inferior.'

gauges and even micrometers. But this was only the formal skeleton of a course without an ideology to guide it. The schools had a far more important function than to equip their pupils with a few elementary skills; they also had to instil an attitude of mind which would be conducive to effective performance of their future tasks in life. The lower classes needed a *Mythos*, and they got what they needed, the Mythos of Muscularity. Luckily they already had this in a rudimentary form, which the modern schools have been able to promote into the modern cult of physical (as distinct from mental) prowess. The English love of sport was traditional, and nowhere stronger than in the lower classes. The modern schools were not breaking with the past, they were building on it, when they encouraged their pupils to value physical strength, bodily discipline, and manual dexterity. Handicrafts, gymnastics, and games have become the core of the curriculum. This enlightened approach has achieved a double purpose. Appreciation of manual work has been cultivated, and leisure made more enjoyable. Of the two, education for leisure has been the most important. More capable pupils have been trained to participate in active games which they can continue to play when they leave school; and the others who form the great majority have been given heightened appreciation of boxing, football, and other sports displayed before them nightly on the screens in their own homes. They esteem physical achievement almost as highly as we of the upper classes esteem mental.

Secondly, the adult education movement has, in its maturity, not only maintained and enlarged the regional centres but has arranged for everyone, irrespective of previous results, to attend there for a periodic intelligence check at intervals of five years.

Tests can be even more frequent at the behest of the individual. A few remarkable changes of I.Q. both up and down, have occurred in middle life. Widely publicized in the popular newspapers, the reports have given new heart to many an ambitious technician. Now that psychiatric treatment is freely available in every workplace, many people with emotional blocks to the realization of their potential have been fully cured.

Thirdly, even when they have abandoned hope themselves, all parents have been solaced by the knowledge that, however low their own I.Q., their child (or grandchild) will have the chance to enter the meritocracy. The solace is a real one. Psychologists have shown that parents, whose own ambitions are thwarted, invariably displace those ambitions on to their children. They are satisfied if they think that their own child may achieve what they could not achieve themselves. 'Do as I wish, not as I do,' they say. The relationship can even be expressed in quantitative terms: according to the well-known principle of compensating aspirations, the greater the frustrations parents experience in their own lives, the greater their aspirations for their children. Almost from the moment when they fail their first intelligence tests at school, children can comfort themselves that one day they will have offspring who will do better; and even when it is dismally clear from teachers' reports that the offspring too are dull, there are still the grandchildren.[1] Personal failings are not so painful if there is a vision of vicarious triumph. As long as all have opportunity to rise through the schools, people can

1. Three-generation interlocking of aspirations in the extended family was discussed in an interesting way by Michael Young in 'The Role of the Extended Family in Channeling Aspirations,' *British Journal of Sociology*, March 1967. Note the earliness of the date.

believe in immortality: they have a second chance through the younger generation. Also, the more children, the more second chances, which helps to account for the higher birth-rate in the second half of last century, after the reforms.

The fourth saving feature has been the very stupidity which has assigned the lower classes to their present status. A common mistake of some sociologists is to impute to the lower orders the same capacity as themselves – a way of thinking akin to anthropomorphism. Sociologists would naturally be aggrieved were they to be denied their proper status. But the lower classes are the objects of study, not the students. The attitude of mind is quite different. People of low intelligence have sterling qualities: they go to work, they are conscientious, they are dutiful to their families. But they are unambitious, innocent, and incapable of grasping clearly enough the grand design of modern society to offer any effective protest. Some are sulkily discontented, without being too sure what to do about it, and find their way to the psychologist or the priest. Most are not, for they know not what is done to them.

3. PIONEERS OF DIRTY WORK

The fifth, and most important, saving feature has been the application of scientific selection to industry. In the previous chapter I showed how promotion by merit gradually replaced promotion by seniority – how the grammar school and university streams were eventually extended into working life. I will now deal with the treatment of the secondary modern stream.

The modern schools have been reproduced in industry just as surely as the grammar schools, and with consequences just as far-reaching. The starting-point is again the Hitler war. In the early years of that war the methods of distributing recruits were almost as haphazard as in industry. Only after several disasters was a more sensible practice adopted, described as follows in the words of a leading Command Psychiatrist in one of the official histories of the war:

In allocating personnel, the basic principle should be that no man is to be employed on work which is definitely above, or, on the other hand, definitely below his ability. Any other method of allotment is wasteful of ability, or destructive of unit efficiency.[1]

What wise and far-sighted words!

By the end of the war the instruction was obeyed and very few men entering the Forces were assigned to any branch until their intelligence and aptitudes had been ascertained as accurately as the crude methods of the time allowed. Much greater efficiency was obtained in the utilization of manpower when the stupid were kept together, and the lesson was not lost on some of the better brains in civilian industry. This was long before advertisers began to include 'State I.Q.' (soon shortened to S.I.Q.) in their copy; and longer still before H.Q. (at Eugenics House) supplied I.Q. certificates to authorized inquirers by teleprinter. The flower of that experiment of the 1940s was the Pioneer Corps. When this indispensable body of hewers and drawers was confined to men with I.Q.s below the line required to get them into the Intelligence Corps, the rise in efficiency was spectacular. The morale of these dull-witted men was better. They were no longer daunted by having superior people to compete with. They were amongst

1. F. A. E. Crew, F.R.S. *The Army Medical Services.* H.M.S.O., 1955.

their equals – they had more equal opportunities since they had more limited ones – and they were happier, had fewer mental breakdowns, *and* were harder working. The Army had learnt the lesson of the schools: that people can be taught more easily, and get on better, when they are classed with people of more or less equal intelligence, or lack of it.

Not until the 1960s did this same lesson strike home in civil life. Intelligent people used to ask themselves what they thought was a profound poser: 'Who', they asked, 'will do the dirty work in the future commonwealth?' Those who knew the right answer apparently said: 'Machines, of course; they will be the robots of the future.' It was a good answer as far as it went, but, in view of the many jobs which can never be taken over by machinery, at best a partial one. Then as they became aware of the new and revolutionary developments in intelligence testing, aptitude testing, and vocational selection, managements realized that a permanent peace-time Pioneer Corps was a practical possibility. At first tentatively, they suggested the correct answer to the old question: 'Who will do the dirty work?' The correct answer was: 'Why, men who like doing it, of course.'

They could see the need for a kind of permanent civilian Pioneer Corps, men with large muscles and small brains (selected by other men with small muscles and large brains) who were not only good at emptying dustbins and heaving loads but liked doing it. They were never to be asked to do more than they were proved to be fit for. They were never to be forced to mix with anyone who made them feel foolish by emptying dustbins more quickly or, what was worse at that time, by consigning all dustbins to the rubbish-heap – a sure sign either of mental deficiency or genius. As I say, progressive managements were very tentative and even a little shamefaced. They were easily put off by references to Mr Huxley's gammas and Mr Orwell's proles. The managers did not see that these two gentlemen had both been attacking not equal opportunity, but the effects of conditioning and propaganda. By these means even intelligent people were to be brought to accept their fate as manual workers. We know that in the long run this is impossible, and in the short run absurdly wasteful and frustrating. The only good manual workers, we know, are those who have not the ability for anything better. Enlightened modern methods have nothing in common with these brave new worlds. But at first not all managers realized that so signally to square efficiency with justice, and order with humanity, was nothing less than a new stage in the ascent of man, brought within his reach by the early advances in the social sciences.

The Pioneer Corps was the essential counterpart of the administrative class in the civil service; its historical significance is as great as that. The success of open competition in government employment established the principle that the most responsible posts should be filled by the most able people; the Pioneers that the least responsible jobs should be filled by the least able people. In other words, a society in which power and responsibility were as much proportioned to merit as education. The civil service won acceptance far more easily – no one wanted to be blown up by hydrogen bombs or starved of foreign exchange because something less than the finest brains were ensconced in Whitehall. The Pioneers encountered far more opposition. The community of principle governing the civil service and the

Pioneers was not at once recognized. The objectors, amongst them a growing number of socialists, complained of 'indignity'. A vague word, to conceal a vague concept. The brute fact is that the great majority of minds were still thinking in pre-merit terms.

In the dark England of the distant past it made the best of sense to plead for equality. In the main way that counts, in their brain-power, the industrial workers, or the peasantry, or whoever it might be, were as good as their masters. What the anti-Pioneers did not realize was that the gradual shift from inheritance to merit as the ground of social selection was making (and has finally made) nonsense of all their loose talk of the equality of man. Men, after all, are notable not for the equality, but for the inequality, of their endowment. Once all the geniuses are amongst the élite, and all the morons amongst the workers, what meaning can equality have? What ideal can be upheld except the principle of equal status for equal intelligence? What is the purpose of abolishing inequalities in nurture except to reveal and make more pronounced the inescapable inequalities of Nature?

The decisive fact was the happiness of the Pioneers, or hand-workers, as they were at first called to distinguish them from brain-workers. No one wanted to flood the chronic wards of the mental hospitals, yet that is just what industry had for many years been doing by setting sub-standard people to perform tasks beyond their reach. No one wanted, least of all the socialists, to cause unnecessary suffering. The principle – 'From each according to his capacity, neither more nor less' – was empirically justified. The workers were more content, and so, for the same reason, were the large middle-classes with I.Q.s broadly between 100 and 125. It was shown time and time again by the psychologists that to put a highly intelligent man on a routine job was as disastrous – reflected as it was in sickness, absenteeism, and neurosis[1] – as the obverse. Matching of intelligence and job in the various streams of society was everywhere demonstrated as the highest expression of both efficiency and humanity; as the very engine of productivity at the same time as the liberator of mankind. Without the scientific study of human relations in industry, resentment against the declining status of the lower classes, and the widening gap between them and the upper classes, would have disrupted society long ago.

4. THE NEW UNEMPLOYMENT

The axiom of modern thought is that people are unequal, and the ensuing moral injunction that they should be accorded a station in life related to their capacities. By dint of a long struggle, society has at last been prevailed upon to conform: the mentally superior have been raised to the top and the mentally inferior lowered to the bottom. Both wear clothes that fit them, and, as I say, it is doubtful whether the lower classes would have

1. An investigation made just after the Hitler war was, to judge from the press, given insufficient attention at the time. 'The women, who were on jobs requiring skill that did not correspond with their intelligence, had a higher incidence of recent definite neurosis than those on jobs whose skill requirements did correspond: the incidence of neurosis was equally high, irrespective of whether the skill required by the job was too high or too low compared with the worker's intelligence.' Russell Fraser. *The Incidence of Neurosis amongst Factory Workers*. Industrial Health Research Board Report, No. 90, H.M.S.O., 1947. An earlier report of the same Board said that 'severe boredom is usually found associated with more than average intelligence'. I.H.R.B., No. 77, H.M.S.O., 1937.

become so docile unless they had, in fact, found the clothes comfortable. The psychologists gave the world the means of identifying people without ability. But, burdened in this way, what work were they to do? It was no use having a Pioneer Corps unless there was a job for it.

In my own special period, that is before 1963, few contemporary observers were aware that economic progress threatened to produce a new kind of selective unemployment. The trend was visible enough, if they had but looked, but this for the most part they signally failed to do.[1] Or rather they noticed one trend, that of increasing mechanization, but not its inescapable human consequences. They knew that the prime purpose of machinery was to save labour, but did not ask – what kind of labour? Mass unemployment which afflicted the clever and the stupid alike was the kind that people understood; this other kind of sub-intellectual unemployment was still hidden from all but the most discerning.

Following what was called the 'industrial revolution', when processes previously performed by hand were gradually taken over by machines, hand-work was far from being rendered redundant: machinofacture and manufacture proceeded side by side. Early machinery was a godsend to the stupid. It still had to be operated by hand, and repetitive machine-minding was well within the compass of low-grade employees, unskilled or semi-skilled. In a fairly typical mid-twentieth-century factory there was a division between the skilled men and the rest. On the one side were the trained

1. One notable exception was Sir George Thomson, F.R.S., in his book *The Foreseeable Future*, 1955. See particularly the section on 'The Future of the Stupid'.

designers and draughtsmen, the administrators and inspectors, the maintenance men and setters who provided, supervised, and repaired the machinery. On the other were the operators who fed the machine with material, pressed a few simple levers in response to a few simple signals, and extracted the material after processing; or who added a component to an assembly moving forward in a batch or on a belt. In the course of time this division became sharper and sharper, reproducing the division in society itself, with the technical staff being constantly upgraded as the machinery in their care became more complex, and the routine operators being constantly downgraded as the work for which they were responsible became more simple.

More and more was demanded of the skilled men, less and less of the unskilled, until finally there was no need for unskilled men at all. Their work was merely routine, and so it could by definition be progressively taken over and performed by mechanical means. The more simplified a job became, the more easily could it be done by a machine which would feed itself with material, press the lever, and extract the finished article. Semi-automatic became fully automatic. Displacement of low-grade labour became very rapid after the Hitler war with the development of electronics, and especially of servo-mechanisms well-suited to direct industrial processes broken down into their simplest components. So marked was the progress that a new word – 'automation' – was coined for the old business of mechanization in the new form it was taking.

Displacement of labour did not at first show itself openly. The trade unions naturally did not make any distinction between clever and stupid; to them men whose jobs had been forfeit to technical change were members to be protected like any other, and they insisted that people whose jobs were taken away from them by labour-saving machinery should not be dismissed but kept on to do some quite unnecessary work, perhaps merely watching instead of 'minding' the robot at its work. The more intelligent members of the unions did not recognize that it was only the low-calibre workers incapable of doing any complicated work whose interests were menaced; sharing the general egalitarian view that one man was much like another, they identified themselves with the redundant, and supported the unions' attempts to prevent dismissals. The employers often acquiesced for the sake of good relations with their staff, or because they thought it was their responsibility, rather than the State's, to care for 'weaker brethren'. It took a very long time for employers to become fully conscious of the need to reduce labour costs to a minimum, and, until then, they did not know how heavy was the load of passengers they were carrying on their pay-roll. As late as the 1950s a large force of low-grade unskilled workers were constantly drifting in to one employment and out to another, always on the move because they were not capable of holding down a steady job anywhere. Millions changed jobs every year. The employer was perhaps aware that his labour turnover was high, but since he did not as yet test the capacity of new recruits, he had no way of knowing that the primary reason was that most had not the minimum ability required for the work. As people were not, in a period of 'full employment', registered as unemployed, except for the odd period now and then, no one appreciated the existence of this vast floating army. Very few of those endlessly moving were in fact making any adequate return for the wages they received.

Many for whom there was no place in industry came to rest in routine clerical work, or in distribution. That was a happy solution, though not a permanent one. Mechanization, starting in the factory, did not end there: offices and shops were also invaded. In the middle of the century book-keepers and typists were still common in offices; by the last quarter they had almost disappeared. Accounts were the responsibility of calculating machines and typists were no longer needed as intermediaries between the spoken and the written word. As for shops, in the middle of the century they still employed millions of people; twenty-five years later, although shop assistants had not by any means disappeared, there were certainly less of them. The large shop with its more economical use of staff had supplanted many smaller ones, the speedy spread of self-service in something like its modern form had reduced the number of assistants needed, and piped distribution of milk, tea, and beer was extending rapidly.

5. DOMESTIC SERVANTS AGAIN

The Clauson Committee, which reported in 1988, took the view that by that date about a third of all adults were unemployable in the ordinary economy. The complexity of civilization had grown beyond them; owing to lack of intelligence, they could not find niches in the ordinary occupational structure and needed some form of sheltered employment. What was to be done with them? There was only one possible answer. The people who had ended their school lives either in the schools for the educationally sub-normal or in the lower streams of secondary modern schools were only capable of meeting one need: for personal service. For instance, most of them could, if carefully prepared in Government Training Centres and carefully supervised thereafter, serve in public restaurants and places of entertainment, in transport and as caretakers.

That was a start. But as Lord Clauson foresaw, the lower classes would only be fully employed when large numbers of them were engaged in personal service not only outside the home, but in it. His recommendations were hotly contested in Parliament and on the hustings. But what other way was there? The critics had few constructive proposals to make. The absurdity was that many highly intelligent people were wasting much of their time performing purely menial tasks for themselves. A well-endowed person was given a long education at the expense of the State, first at a grammar school and then at a university, and when he came down he was entrusted with a highly responsible post in industry or commerce. His work should have claimed his full energies and his leisure be used for recuperation. But what happened? He spent many valuable hours not at the job for which he had been so elaborately trained, but trailing around the self-service stores buying the odd packet of potatoes or bucket of frozen fish, cleaning his flat, or cooking the fish, or making his bed. I say 'he' but of course the waste was much more widespread for the highly intelligent and hence highly educated woman. After marriage she was not permitted, such was the prevailing anarchy, to carry on the work she could so well do for society; instead, she had to pretend that she had never had a higher education at all, and try to accustom herself to behaving as though household drudgery was the proper reward for *cum laude*, in the same way as a mere secondary modern girl. That was the point – there was no need for much of the drudgery to fall to the lot of the intelligent, it was much better left to the person who would not regard it as drudgery at all because she was not capable of doing anything higher. Drudgery for the one hundred and thirty could be joy for the eighty-five. Had nothing been learnt from the Pioneers?

The critics protested that domestic service was not just service, it was servile. They had tradition on their side, but did not seem to realize how short-lived this was. For thousands of years it was the accepted thing for the upper class to have servants. They only vanished between the demise of the old aristocracy and the birth of the new; in the egalitarian age when no man was held worthy enough to deserve service from his fellows; in the interim period when no one was sure of anything except that Jack was supposed to be as good as his master. When the conditions fostering egalitarianism passed away, there was no further need for this one of its manifestations. Domestic service could be restored once it was again accepted that some men were superior to others; and done without resentment because the inferior knew their betters had a great part to play in the world and beyond, and were glad to identify with them and wait on them. Far better to perform a recognized and valuable service for an important person than to languish on the dole. Naturally, there were safeguards. No one wanted to see a return of the abuses which used to exist in the nineteenth century. All domestic servants were formally enrolled in the Home Help Corps – it topped the ten million mark by the turn of the century – and every private employer had to pay the wages laid down; provide sanitary living-space; release the servant two nights a week to attend a sports club run by the Corps; pay for a refresher course every summer; and not demand more than forty-eight hours a week except with permission from the local office. As far as female servants are concerned, the new arrangement has on the whole worked well, even if morons have sometimes done very silly things to air-conditioners. The trouble has been the men. Despite all experiments at the Corps research centres, no really adequate modern counterpart has been found for the butler and the footman of old. Male unemployment has been higher than female for forty years or more.

6. SUMMARY

Under the new dispensation the division between the classes has been sharper than it used to be under the old, the status of the upper classes higher, and that of the lower classes lower. In this chapter I have discussed some of the repercussions upon the social structure. Any historian knows that class conflict was endemic throughout pre-merit times, and, in the light of past experience, might perhaps expect that any rapid diminution in the status of one class would necessarily aggravate such conflict. The question is: why have the changes of the last century not led to such an issue? Why has society been so stable in spite of the widening gulf between the bottom and the top?

The cardinal reason is that stratification has been in accord with a principle of merit, generally accepted at all levels of society. A century ago the lower classes had an ideology of their own – in essentials the same as that which has now become paramount – and were able to use it as much to advance themselves as to attack their superiors. They denied the right of the upper classes to their position. But in the new conditions the lower classes no longer have a distinctive ideology in conflict with the ethos of society, any more than the lower orders used to in the heyday of feudalism. Since bottom agrees with top that merit should reign, they can only cavil at the means by which the choice has been made, not at the standard which all alike espouse. So much, so good. Yet we would be failing in our duty as sociologists did we not point out that such widespread recognition of merit as the arbiter may condemn to helpless despair the many who have no merit, and do so all the more surely because the person so condemned, having too little wit to make his protest against society, may turn his anger against, and so cripple, himself.

The situation has been saved by the Mythos of Muscularity, adult education, displacement of ambitions on to children, and natural stupidity. Above all by extending into adult life the main lineaments of the educational system. If, in the adult world as much as in the school, the stupid are kept together, they are not reminded at every turn of their inferiority. By the standards of the group in which they move and have their being they are, indeed, not stupid; here they are amongst their equals; they can even, in a modest way, shine in the display of their more commendable attributes. When they are amongst their equals, the great society does not press harshly upon them, nor resentments linger. They have the respect of their fellows in their own intelligence-grade. This class solidarity, provided it is not coloured with a rebellious ideology, can be, I would say certainly has been, a most valuable aid to the cohesion of society. For a time all was threatened by a species of technological unemployment, but once the Home Helps Corps was firmly established, what looks like a permanent and most constructive outlet was provided for the graduates of our modern schools.

It is not unfair to give some credit to Crosland, Taylor, Dobson, Clauson, and all the other founders of modern society for the solid way in which they built. But if we take for granted the permanence of the structure, we do so at our peril. Any sociological analysis, of the kind I have attempted in this chapter, shows full well how much depends upon an intricate system of checks and balances. Discontent cannot be totally removed even from our rational society. Here and there lurks the inferior paranoid man, harbouring resentment against some monstrous injustice which he imagines has been done to him; the romantic who hankers after the disorder of the past; the servant who feels isolated in her meritorium, even from the children whom she tends.

CHAPTER SIX

FALL OF THE LABOUR MOVEMENT

I. HISTORIC MISSION

THE many followers of Professor Diver hold that political institutions are always secondary to others; merely products, never creators, of the primary institutions in the economic and educational spheres. I do not deny the plausibility of this thesis, and yet at the same time I cannot accept it in its usual formulation. No doubt it is true of the present. But is it of the past? Of the twentieth century in particular? The Cambridge school has achieved nothing if it has not demonstrated the critical importance of the Labour Movement in the era of transition. In a sense, of course, its role was secondary even then. Social change stemmed from the economy, the pressure was international competition, the instrument was education. And yet the need for adaptation had to be translated into a language which people could make their own. The historic mission of the Labour Movement was to win people's minds to the new view of life.

Socialists gained the prize of equal opportunity by preaching equality, and, until the battle was over, there was no harm in that. But once equality of opportunity was a fact, to go on preaching equality was obviously not only unnecessary, it was calculated to undo the very achievement for which Labour could take so much of the credit. Unlike the root-and-branch egalitarians who have continued to erupt spasmodically in the cabals of which the Populists are the heir, the main body of the Movement has meshed smoothly with the new age. The standing of the Movement had to fall along with the standing of manual workers generally, for if it had not, the lower classes would hardly have been induced to accept their lot. We might have had not evolution, but catastrophe. If I am right, an understanding of the last century cannot be complete without appreciating the peculiar function of socialists, in their rise and in their fall.

Improvement in methods of social selection was the condition of progress. But before the harvest could be reaped there was another social revolution to complete, and as profound. All would have been in vain unless select minds had been prepared for their high vocation. Had they been unwilling to shoulder their responsibilities, the new social order would have been stillborn. Everyone had to be imbued with eagerness to rise as high as his abilities justified. Before modern society could reach maturity, ambition had to be forced ever upwards, and the ideology of the people brought into conformity with the needs of the new scientific age.

In effecting this vital psychological change – making discipline voluntary by putting a goad inside the mind – socialism has played an indispensable part. In the beginning there was protestantism. As Weber and Tawney showed long ago, the function of protestantism was to fire the acquisitive urge. The successful adaptation of religion to economic requirements was what made expansion possible in Western Europe and the parts of the world which once formed part of the British Empire. The failure of older religions elsewhere to supply the fuel was likewise the reason for the emergence of the new and linked religions of communism and nationalism,[1] and for the revolutions which accompanied the transition. To make the Russian, Chinese, or Arab mind receptive to turbo-generators, electrostatic wands, and atomic piles, communism in alliance with nationalism was as necessary as a mother to a child. In Britain puritanism-protestantism took the country through the early stages of the first industrial revolution. But beyond a certain point it could not go, until protestantism, through the medium of the nonconformist churches, became transmuted into anglo-socialism, the new evangelical movement, of the sort which held sway in the first half of last century.

The limitation of protestantism was that while it encouraged the acquisition of wealth it did not stress the necessity of social mobility. It even sanctioned the accumulation of wealth with the very motive of hoarding for descendants. In its essentials it was therefore but a compromise, though at that time a necessary one, with the hereditary extremism of the feudal system. The great, though temporary, contribution of socialism was that it picked out one element in the Christian teaching and gave it prominence to the exclusion of all else. It emphasized equality. Christians had, if often in muted

1. Dr Straker has pointed out in his *Studies of World Revolution* the very close similarity between socialism and nationalism-communism. These were both creeds of the underdog, one reacting against the pretensions of superior classes, the other against the pretensions of superior nations. They both started by demanding equality, while in reality striving for superiority of the classes and nations they represented. They were both successful because, amongst the inferior classes and nations, were many intelligent people deprived of recognition for their talents. It is in the long run impossible to keep large numbers of able (as distinct from stupid) people in servitude; they will revolt – the disaster in South Africa is a particularly telling example within living memory.

tones, taught that as all men were the children of God, so were all men equal in the eyes of their Father. To the father, children; to each other, brothers.[1] Socialists developed this doctrine into a powerful weapon. They used the weapon to destroy resistance to change.

'What right', they asked, 'has one man to wealth when another has none, what right has any man to rule over his brother? Is not inequality an affront to the dignity of man?' These notions were the pure milk of the gospel. So influential were they that many early socialists were only won round to accept the need for the fullest opportunities for individual ascent by the brilliant invention of the idea of equality of opportunity. When opportunity was coupled with equality it was made more than respectable; it became the Holy Grail. Socialists did not see that, as it was applied in practice, equality of opportunity meant equality of opportunity to be unequal. This structural blindness was necessary if the socialists were to concentrate with vigour upon opening wide the doors to talent. In practice, as I mentioned earlier, they attacked with most energy the forms of inequality due to inheritance. Death duties, the decay of nepotism, free secondary and university education, the integration of the public schools, wages for children, the abolition of the hereditary House of Lords, these are their most momentous achievements.

I am maintaining that the hereditary principle would never have been overthrown, a psychological change on the vast scale that the economy required never accomplished, without the aid of a new religion – and that

1. An interesting survival is that even the members of A.S.S.E.T. and other technical unions still refer to each other as brothers. There is some justification because identical twins are the only siblings with identical I.Q.s, initially at any rate.

religion was socialism. It undermined resistance in two ways. It dealt, firstly, with the upper caste. After a long struggle the wealthy were, to the greatest extent possible without transferring newborn children straight to residential nurseries,[1] prevented from transmitting privilege to their children. How was this to be done? Parental selfishness had to be socialized – that is, made subordinate to the interests of society. Parents had to be educated to understand it was a sin to seek high positions for stupid children – if they did so, the advantage of the community would be sacrificed to the selfish interests of one small family amongst many. Such a high standard of civilized behaviour has never yet been fully attained. But what ceaseless socialist agitation did was to convince wealthy parents of the futility of *open* resistance. Why were death duties not opposed more strongly, the integration of private schools not opposed to the bitter end? The wealthy could not fight because their morale was sapped by socialist teaching, all the more so when, for the sake of their own survival, the Conservatives quietly came to terms with their opponents: the Conservatives of that day were the supreme example of those who live, as someone said of the Arabs, by stealing each other's washing. Attacked as moral culprits by the socialists, deserted by their own champions, those with inherited wealth eventually succumbed, leaving only a few crazy women to carry on the fight. The holders of power and possessors of wealth need, in

1. Some socialists virtually wanted to go so far. There is on record an interesting statement by a local government officer in 1949 at the high point of socialist success. 'We look forward', he said, 'to the day when children of all social classes will be found in our state nurseries.' Many over-enthusiastic teachers, impatient of parental pretensions, would have agreed with him.

all societies, to have the assurance of the best of moral titles to their fortune. Otherwise no ruling class can rule with the unbounded assurance which is the hidden spring of charisma. In feudal times blood was the unchallenged title to power. In capitalist times wealth was its own title. But as conditions changed, the hereditary rich could no longer hold up their heads. They lost the confidence to rule, and step by step they relinquished power to the self-made and even more notably to the school-made men who had the heavenly support of society's deep-seated moral approval, and hence of their own. The new rulers were those who, according to the new values, deserved to wear the purple mantle.

The second achievement was to instil ambition into the working class. For the socialists nothing succeeded like success in the short run just as, in the long run, nothing failed like success. Every advance towards greater equality of opportunity in education, or towards the widening of opportunity in industry, stimulated aspiration. In the well-adjusted personality ambition lies always close to the surface, ready to stir to life at the caress of hope. Each new opportunity did something to sharpen appetite. Demand, as always, helped to create its own supply.

Until well on into Elizabethan times family succession to jobs was much more common in the lower than in the middle classes. In London or Liverpool the docker's son followed his father's occupation, despite every blandishment of his mistress at school, because he had the absurd idea that it was the finest calling in the world. So did coal-miners' sons in Durham villages, farm-workers' sons in distant parts of Somerset, steel-men at Corby and Scunthorpe. The improvement of communications helped to root out such wickedness by advertising the standards of the wealthy and the glittering lives of thousands of people far beyond his own community to every child in the country. All subjective judgements about the status of different jobs were assimilated to the one national model. In later years, the famous argument by analogy from sport – a shrewd touch this – figured powerfully in the armoury of the adult educators. Would any British technician choose his local football team from the sons of past flyers, whether or not they were the best men? Then why management? Only recently has the argument been twisted round. The reformers ask what, if there is nothing to do but play first-class football, is to happen to all those not good enough to get a place in the team?

The extension of opportunity and the improvement of communication, once they had begun to gather momentum, made psychological transformation possible; they did not make it necessary. Without the ferment of socialist agitation, the working man would have remained sunk in apathy, lacking sufficient drive to take advantage of his great new chances. Every intelligent generation, it seems, must re-discover for itself the resignation with which the ordinary man accepts his lot. The technician is always liable not only to feel that he might as well put up with his job since he has little chance of anything better, but that his son should do likewise. From this apathy he has to be repeatedly rescued by those who have a truer sense of values. Socialism was once the liberator. It fought against complacency. It taught the technician that he was the equal of the Corporation President, who therefore had no right to his greater wealth. By preaching equality, it goaded people with envy, and envy put the spur to competition. When a man determines to excel his superior, he is giving vent, in sublimated form, to his infantile wishes to surpass his father. A profound energy is released and harnessed to a constructive purpose. When coupled with brain-power, this energy is irresistible. But it had to be unlocked, and socialism was the key. If envy has become a public virtue instead of a private vice, we know to whom credit must be given.

The great dilemma of industrial society is that ambition is aroused, in lesser measure but still aroused, in the minds of stupid children and of their parents as well as in the minds of the intelligent. This is inevitable since no one has been able to foresee with complete accuracy where ability is going to sprout. Everyone has to be ambitious so that no one with talents of a high order shall fail to make use of them. Yet when ambition is crossed with stupidity it may do nothing besides foster frustration. Hence the following of intellectual egalitarians. Though they are superior people, they are so much afraid of being envied that they identify themselves with the underdog, and speak for him. They demand that equality be more than opportunity: they demand equality in power, education, and income; they demand that equality be made the ruling principle of the social order; they demand that the unequal be treated *as though* they were equal.

Socialism ceased to be an accelerator, and became a brake. It achieved its mission when first education, and then industry, had been so much reorganized that nearly all the able people in the country were concentrated in the upper classes. The Labour Party could no longer be the force it had been once the classes it represented had lost the intelligent from their ranks. The Party's standing in the country was bound to suffer. Another blow was the decline of parliament. Redistribution of intelligence is the cause of deterioration in the House of Commons, as well as in the Labour Party; the one has reinforced the other.

2. DECLINE OF PARLIAMENT

The British genius – if such a word can be applied to a nation which is in intelligence almost as much a cross-section of mankind as any other – the British genius is pouring new beer into old bottles. We believe in evolution, and not revolution, precisely because we know that change can be all the more rapid when, on the surface, there is no change at all. It has happened with the Commonwealth. It has happened with the monarchy. It has happened with the Labour Movement. It has happened with parliament.

Democracy, in so far as it meant that power resided in an all-powerful elected legislature, was a typical product of the transition from caste to class; its basic assumption of one man, one vote, was egalitarian. The mother of a problem family submerged in Brighouse and Spenborough had the same vote as a Beatrice Webb. The parliamentary system, as Maine[1] put it, was 'listening nervously at one end of a speaking-tube which receives at its other end the suggestions of a lower intelligence'.

In feudal times the country was governed by a ruling caste. In modern times we have a casteless society and the country is governed by a ruling *class*. In between it was governed by neither caste nor class, rather by a combination of both. For hundreds of years, blood shared power with brain; long after withering of the hereditary principle had begun to concentrate ability at

1. *Popular Government*, 1886.

the top, each class, however lowly, still possessed its superior men and women. In these circumstances, universal suffrage was only facing the facts. To give equal weight to each class was as good a way as any other of securing a parliament of talent. The textile workers, the miners, the steel workers, the farmers, and other groups elected from their own ranks men of above-average intelligence. Their M.P.s were fit to rule.

The supremacy of parliament was no sooner assured than it began to be threatened by the ever-growing complexity of the state. The men shall we say of Campbell Bannerman's administration, or even of the first Labour Government under Ramsay MacDonald, were worthy of their place. The issues were still so simple that the intelligent amateur – the proud status of the ancient M.P.s – could make a wise decision. Under conditions of primitive technology this was true. By the time of the Butler Government the ordinary business of state had become so extraordinary that the amateur, however gifted, could do little more than go through the motions of grappling with it. Even to go through motions was so much a full-time job that M.P.s could not easily make up their income from outside work. This was rendered more and more necessary, while less and less possible, by one of the more fortunate victories of egalitarian sentiment – the limiting of M.P.s' salaries. The able could less and less afford to go into parliament and the quality of the Labour and other Parties suffered in consequence. Intelligence has always followed power: when power slipped away to the civil service, the outstanding men tiptoed after it: when the outstanding men left politics, fewer were left behind to resist the encroachment of Whitehall. Nowadays double-firsts from Oxford and Cambridge do not regard a political career as either their interest or their duty. Interest does not bid them wait upon a fickle electorate; duty calls them to serve society by filling a post of the highest responsibility, which parliament, for ninety-eight per cent of M.P.s, can no longer offer. Modern Gladstones are at Harwell. Another cause of the decline is that the lower classes, although progressively denuded of ability, have not stopped electing their own kind. They have clung to their democratic rights, with the result that the level of I.Q. in parliament has fallen progressively. The elected representatives of the common people no longer have the brains; they no longer wield the power.

To cope with this problem two main alternative solutions have been proposed, the first revolutionary, the second evolutionary. The 'revolutionaries' have demanded that form should be brought into line with reality and either parliament abolished or election made dependent on an I.Q. qualification. They have also sought proportional representation, whereby the number of votes a man has would be proportional to his intelligence. All this was surely short-sighted. As our forbears said, no one but the wearer knows where the shoe is pinching. Whenever decisions cause suffering, the ordinary man should be able to express his grievance to his M.P.[1] When this right exists, the civil service, and even the social scientists, are kept ever alert. Moreover, simple issues arise from time to time on which the opinion of the ordinary man (when advised by the competent authorities) is as valuable as the opinion of the meritocracy, and on these rare occasions

1. In the way that Beatrice Webb, that wise woman, would have approved: 'we have little faith in the "average sensual man", we do not believe that he can do much more than describe his grievances, we do not think that he can prescribe the remedies'. *Our Partnership.*

we lose nothing by giving the House of Commons the chance to air its views.

By a typically British compromise the purpose of the revolutionaries has been partly achieved not by abolishing the Commons but by reconstituting the Lords. Thorough-going reform was for many years opposed by members of the Labour Party on the significant ground that once the House of Lords ceased to be a hereditary chamber its prestige would be so high as to challenge the Commons. Better, they said, to let the Lords die. In the prevailing mental climate, the objection (however well-founded) could not permanently be sustained. The hereditary principle was too indefensible. A socialist spokesman of the fifties put the more enlightened view when he said:

It is important to remember exactly what Labour's objection to the present House of Lords really is. It does not stem primarily from the weakness or unfairness of the system of creating peers so much as from the absurdity of the inherited element.[1]

The Labour Party ended up as active for reform as their opponents. The banning of hereditary peers, the restriction of membership to life peers, women as well as men, chosen from among the most eminent people in the Kingdom, the payment of generous *honoraria* – these reforms, starting in 1958 and continued over the next twenty years, eventually made the upper chamber into a body far more influential than its junior partner. Selection largely replaced election. Skipping all the intermediate stages of democracy (as some countries have jumped straight from railways to rockets), instrument of the aristocracy was by one brilliant stroke made

1. Anthony Wedgwood Benn, M.P. *The Privy Council as a Second Chamber.* Fabian Society, 1957.

THE RISE OF THE MERITOCRACY

instrument of the meritocracy. The hold of the Lords of Parliament was assured when by a constitutional convention the Ministry of Education was in all cabinets reserved to the upper chamber. The House is now quite as distinguished as the Central Committee which contains the appointed, self-perpetuating rulers of Communist China – the House of Lords is the central committee of our élite class.

The other way of evolution was to compensate for the inevitable weakness of parliament by strengthening the civil service. Nourished by first-class selection in the schools and first-class training in the universities, fertilized by new techniques of research and administration, buttressed by the tradition and camaraderie of more than a century's unselfish devotion to duty, the collective competence of the civil service has, with only a few setbacks, continued to soar. Confronted with this composite wisdom, nearly all amateur politicians in Ministerial office have been content to take the glory and abandon the power. The dangerous exception is the politician so stupid or so vain that he does not even recognize his own incompetence. He may, like Queen Victoria, actually demand that his nominal power be made real. Part of the lore of the civil service consists in the accumulated knowledge of how to defeat such pretension.[1] I am speaking of thirty years ago. Fortunately

1. Even in the great days of the House, the civil servant was very much the power behind the scenes. Here is one piece of advice to those drafting answers to Parliamentary Questions. 'It might be said, cynically, but with some measure of truth, that the perfect reply to an embarrassing question in the House of Commons is one that is brief, appears to answer the question completely, if challenged can be proved to be accurate in every word, gives no opening for awkward "supplementaries", and discloses really nothing.' Dale, H. E. *The Higher Civil Service.*

there have been no Prince Alberts in the parliaments of this century. As conflict in society has been reduced, the civil servants, now that they no longer need keep aloof, have taken a more active part in politics to make up for the devitalization of the two-party system. Both they and the vital House of Lords belong to a meritocracy of growing power. The House of Commons has not yet followed the horse – let us hope it never will – let us hope it has now, like the monarchy, found a permanent niche in the constitution, the old merging in the new, the new in the old, on a higher level.

3. THE TECHNICIANS

The historian's puzzle is why the Labour Party lasted so long: what could more perfectly illustrate the principle of social inertia? Like democracy itself, the Labour Party was a reaction against the feudal tradition. It arose out of the old working class as it was called, which had such solidarity because its name belied it: it was not so much class as caste. Universal suffrage in the nineteenth and twentieth centuries gave political power to the workers. They held together and, advancement of other kinds being partly denied to them, made full use of this political power to challenge high-caste authority. Able and ambitious leaders whose individual ascent was barred by the hereditary system bent their efforts to improve the lot of their class as a whole, their class and not just themselves within it! A whole class was to rise, quite without respect to the capacity of its members!

They formed a mighty army, until by their very success, the socialist achievement of which I spoke earlier, they stormed the citadel and opened the gates to talent.

Victory reduced the army to brigades, platoons and then, at last, to lone snipers. By the 1960s the outstanding children of manual fathers were no longer gravely handicapped by their origin. On the strength of sheer individual merit they could rise up the social ladder as far as their ability would stretch. This was a boon to them and a boon as well to their parents. But for the working class as a whole the victory was a defeat. Sated by conquest, the class began to crumble from within. More and more parents began to harbour ambitions for their children rather than for their class. The cult of the child became the drug of the people; inspired by hope, vitalized by ambition, the whole nation began to advance as never before from the moment that the Labour Party came to a standstill.

The Labour Party made the inevitable compromise with the new society it had done so much to create: it ceased to exist. Fewer and fewer electors, however brawny, responded instinctively to the appeal of 'labour'. Drawn upwards by their aspirations for their children, all but the lumpenproletariat, to re-adopt a term still in vogue in the first half of the century, conceived of themselves as a cut above the labourer at the bottom of the heap. 'Workers' became a discredited word. The canny leaders of the mid-century Labour Party (which still contained many highly competent men) recognized full well the need for change. They scrapped the appeal to working-class solidarity and concentrated on the middle class, partly to capture new sections of the electorate, more to keep pace with their own supporters who had, in their outlook, moved upwards from their point of origin. One of the symptoms of rampant ambition was the upgrading by name alone of occupations which could not be upgraded in any other way. We no longer have to be so hypocritical. We can recognize inferiority and dare to label it so. But in those days rat-catchers were called 'rodent officers', sanitary inspectors 'public health inspectors', and lavatory cleaners 'amenities attendants'. Employers conformed to the changing *mores* by dismissing their 'workers' and hiring none but technicians, clothed in white coats instead of dungarees. The Labour Party finally made the same adjustment. 'Labour' was a millstone; 'worker' was taboo; but 'technician', what magic was there! And so the modern Technicians Party was born, catering in the broadest possible manner for technicians by hand and by brain.

The trade unions followed. The Transport and General Workers Union became the Transport and General Technicians Union; the National Union of General and Municipal Workers, the National Union of General and Municipal Technicians. This did not altogether save them from the competition of that other great general union, the Association of Supervisory Staffs and Engineering Technicians, which enjoyed the advantage of correct name and status from the start. The Mineworkers became the Mine Technicians (still a force in the early days of the Technicians Party), the Woodworkers the Wood Technicians, the Textile Workers the Textile Technicians, the Clerical Workers the Office Technicians, and so forth. Likewise the Technical Unions Congress and the Technicians' Education Association. Higher grades had to notch up their own classification in order to maintain the vital differentials of status. Laboratory technicians could not, for instance, retain such a designation without being confused with charring technicians. They styled themselves laboratory specialists, and for the same reason certain of the unions (other than A.S.S.E.T.) adopted new names – the Association of Building Technicians, for instance, became the A.B.S. and the Association of Psychological Technicians the A.P.S. The Association of Scientific Workers had, like the House of Lords which its members adorn, to jump over a whole stage in social development. The more so after it had amalgamated with the Association of Local Government Sociologists, it considered A.S.S. not altogether appropriate and so boldly adopted the title of Benefactors – the A.S.B. as it is now justly esteemed far beyond the circles whose immediate work lies in the benefactories and compartment stores.

The high-I.Q. unions have exercised influence in the T.U.C. disproportionate to their numbers, if not yet quite proportionate to their intelligence. They have helped to speed the transformation of work into play as fast as the play of the meritocracy has (for the assessment of income) been converted into work. They have helped to concentrate the attention of the technical unions on adult education of the modern sort. They have exposed the I.Q.-crammers. They led the successful campaign for the adoption of the metric system in weights, measures, and money. They have taught their technical colleagues to take a sober view of the role of the Technicians Party in the modern state. And all the time they have had to battle against the sentimental. The old egalitarianism could not be wiped out overnight, and the sentimentalists have continued to praise the virtues of the good old days and protest, in the name of equality, against every advance towards social justice.

4. ADJUSTMENT IN THE UNIONS

To appreciate how far we have come, cast your mind back to a meeting of the tripartite National Joint Council for Industry, say, in 1950. There sat Ministers of the Crown with representatives of the T.U.C., the F.B.I., and the public corporations. Did any group have more ability than another? Were the trade unionists outmanoeuvred in argument because they left school at thirteen or fourteen while the leaders of private industry had been to Cambridge and the chiefs of the public corporations to Sandhurst? Were the trade union leaders at a disadvantage because they were shoved into a factory at an age when the others were still in short trousers? Obviously not – if anything the advantage was the other way round. The trade unionists not only spoke from longer experience. They included some of the ablest men in the country. The sharing of power between the classes was the natural consequence of sharing the intelligence. These leaders commanded the confidence of the followers from whose ranks they came, and deserved to. Many of them were Ministers in the first, second, third, and fourth Labour Cabinets, before the decline set in. The ability of the miners' leaders was especially high, for in colliery villages there were no other jobs for young men to take and little prospect of promotion to the middle class. It was not fully appreciated in the 1950s and 1960s that these folk-heroes were not being succeeded by others equally able; the children of top trade unionists and Labour Ministers, and of other outstanding working men, were not becoming manual workers themselves. They were in attendance at grammar schools and universities, training for commerce and the professions, very large numbers of them even going to public schools. The children of the Labour leaders were the augurs of the future.

Contrast the present – think how different was a meeting in the 2020s of the National Joint Council, which has been retained for form's sake. On the one side sit the I.Q.s of 140, on the other the I.Q.s of 99. On the one side the intellectual magnates of our day, on the other honest, horny-handed workmen more at home with dusters than documents. On the one side the solid confidence born of hard-won achievement; on the other the consciousness of a just inferiority. The trade union-ists' ponderous, carefully rehearsed reflections have no more influence upon their colleagues, if we are frank with ourselves, than a pea-shooter upon an astro-rocket. Primed with their sociological surveys the civil servants know more about the state of opinion in the factories than the stewards who work in them. The union leaders seldom have the insight to see that the courtesy with which they are treated is pure formality. They do not know that instead of the substance of power, they are being flattered by its shadow.

We do not need to ask why. The schools have begun to do their proper job of social selection – that is all. Once the long-called-for reforms were made, none of the ablest children in the country, unless by an unfor-tunate mistake, had to take up manual work. They were trained by something better than the 'Workers Educational Association' (*sic*). Twenty years after 1944 the brilliant children of manual workers automatically went to the best grammar schools in their district, from there on to Oxford and Cambridge, and, when they came down, they were eligible for travelling scholar-ships and grants for the Imperial College of Science, the Inns of Court, and the Administrative Staff College.

The Keir Hardies of later generations have been the star civil servants, physicists, psychologists, chemists, business executives, and music critics of their day.

Amongst children who left school for manual jobs in the 1940s one in twenty still had I.Q.s over 120; in the 1950s – after the Act was working – there was one in fifty, by the 1970s only one in a thousand. By the last quarter of the century, the supply of really capable working men to fill the top union posts had dried up completely, and long before that, the fall in quality amongst Union M.P.s and branch and workshop officials, especially amongst the younger men, had become very marked indeed. I should say that the rule of promotion by seniority, to which the unions remained attached, was not such a brake as it was in industry because the older officials were on the whole more able. Intelligence is, of course, by no means the only quality required by a union leader; they also need belligerence, doggedness, and capacity for hard work. But although intelligence is not the only quality, it is a necessary one, and the new leaders have been dreadfully handicapped by its absence.

How, then, have the unions kept going at all? They have been saved by three kinds of adjustment – by the strengthening of their appointed staff, simplification of their functions, and enhancement of their respectability. First, the weaknesses of the electoral method have been partially offset, in the trade unions as in parliament, by reinforcing the appointed 'civil service'. Very few university graduates have been elected as officials of manual unions, but increasingly, if far too slowly,[1] the executive committees, conscious of the ever-

1. The Cooperative Movement was also very slow to react to educational change. A report in the 1930s commented that the

growing complexity of the economy, impressed by the growing prestige of the universities, and aware of the need to make as good a show as possible with the employers and the government, have themselves appointed graduates to their research, production, and public relations departments. The Labour Party led in welcoming as M.P.s men from Winchester and other élite schools and then from the universities to replace the able manual workers who did not exist any more; by 1960 hardly any of the Party's leaders had been manual workers – a great change from 1924. After a time-lag the Unions did likewise with their officials. The universities have responded with special courses for suitable candidates who, despite high I.Q.s, are tactful enough to suffer fools gladly – a very necessary quality this for the advisers of union executives. The notable sandwich course at the Leeds Institute of Technology prescribes a period in the ranks to gain practical experience; union and management cadets work happily together on the factory floor. The unions have incorporated into their top echelons many graduates who if not of the first rank are still good second-raters in the 115–120 range.

The unions have been preserved by men like Lord Wiffen. To appreciate the excellence of his qualifications one need do no more than compare his career with that of Ernest Bevin, who had no education worth the name.

Cooperative Movement 'has failed to use even the trained ability which is made available for it by the present educational system. Even the advantages of secondary education have not been realized, and recruitment from the universities is almost unknown.' Carr-Saunders, A. M., Sargant, Florence P., and Peers, R. *Consumers Cooperation in Great Britain.*

Lord Wiffen
(Born 9 August 1957,
Bradford.
Father, spinner)

Mr Ernest Bevin
(Born 9 March 1881,
Winsford, Somerset.
Father, farm labourer)

5–11	A Stream Primary School. I.Q. 120	5–11	Learnt to read and write at village school
11	11-plus exam. I.Q. 121	11	Left school to take job as farm boy
13	Bradford Grammar School. I.Q. 119	13	Kitchen boy, Bristol
14	Ditto.	14	Grocer's errand boy
15	Ditto.	15	Van boy
16	Sixth form. I.Q. 118	16	Tram conductor, then van boy again
18	State scholarship, Cambridge University. I.Q. 120. Subsequently 2nd class B.Sc. (Sociology) and M.Sc. (Mental Testing)	18	Drayman
28	Lecturer on Human Relations in Industry. Acton Technical College. I.Q. 123	28	Secretary, Bristol Right to Work Committee
29	Commonwealth Fellow Harvard University. I.Q. 115	29	Secretary, Bristol Carmen's Branch of the Dock, Wharf, Riverside & General Labourers Union
32	Deputy Research Officer, United Textile Factory Technicians Union. I.Q. 115	32	Assistant National Organizer of Union
34	Ditto.	34	National Organizer of Union

41 Research Officer of Union I.Q. 114	41 General Secretary, Transport and General Workers Union
59 K.C.T.U.C., Secretary of Union. Member of General Council. I.Q. 116	59 Minister of Labour
64 Raised to peerage. I.Q. 116	64 Foreign Secretary
72 Chairman, Education Committee T.U.C. I.Q. 112	
76 Assistant Lecturer, Acton Technical College (where he now is). I.Q. 104	

Walter Wiffen and his like have given the leadership which the Bevins once gave to the manual workers.

The second adjustment is that the functions of the trade unions have, in a more sensibly organized society, become almost completely routine, so that there is very little call for initiative or innovation. Shop stewards and local officials are no longer any match for the employers but this matters very little now that any negotiations there are about wages and conditions have become fully centralized at national level, where the influence of the paid staff is predominant. The British Productivity Council has continuously fed the unions with publicity material, films, and cartoons for their members, and the National Joint Council has also become ever more vital since it assumed responsibility for the annual price review. None but trained statisticians can follow the complexities of the review, so the experts employed by the Unions settle the details in discussion with their colleagues from the Central Statistical Office. Up till last

May there had been no 'strike' since the one at Leamington in 1991.

Third, the trade unions, have, like the monarchy, been given an ever more honourable place in the social order. Today there is not a national body of any consequence on which they are unrepresented. Joint consultation has been carried so far by the government as well as by every employer that the unions (except for those in which Populist cliques have gained control) are told, at least a day or two in advance of the public pronouncement, of nearly every important decision. Now that the Royal Order of the T.U.C. has been created and all members of the General Council knighted automatically on election, now that the award of honours to rank-and-file workmen has been multiplied, intelligence and tact have retrieved what might admittedly have become a very ugly situation. The Populists claim there is a basic lack of sympathy between the paid staff and the union rank and file. Any sociologist must recognize the danger. But the remedy is not to move backwards into a past golden only in imagination. The remedy is, as the universities have realized, to perfect the social surveys and opinion polls which are the eyes and ears of the intelligent public.

5. SUMMARY

I started this chapter by praising the socialists for the massive attack they once mounted against the hereditary principle. Without them, castes might never have been replaced by classes, and the old aristocracy never converted into its modern form. But when their mission was accomplished and equality of opportunity achieved, they had to make a far-reaching and sometimes painful adjustment. The main body of the Labour Party, under its new name, became reconciled to the fall in its standing, and to the decline of its special vehicle, parliament. The technical unions were compensated for loss of power by gain in respectability. The organized technicians have become a lesser pillar of our society. But the minority movement of break-away socialists, sometimes working inside the official ranks, sometimes outside, has never been totally destroyed. The Populists can with some justice claim descent from the sentimental egalitarians who have for decades past plagued respectable technicians' leaders as much as they have the government.

Today Lady Avocet likes to compare the meritocracy with the Mohicans who took away the best young men and women from a conquered tribe and reared them as members of their own families. She and her fellows claim that technicians need leaders who share their attitudes of mind because they have been technicians themselves.[1] If they again had an Ernest Bevin to lead them, their morale would again be high because they could identify fully with him and take credit for his deeds. They would again belong to a cohesive society because they would possess a leader who would interpret its

1. In their quarterly journal, *Commonweal*, some Populist writers have taken to sociology too, and advanced a new interpretation of the history of the Hitler war. They are quite right that psychologists in the Royal Navy deliberately left some able men as able seamen, instead of sending them for special training, so that there would be good men in the ranks, knowing the ratings' problems, from whom officers could later be drawn. (See Vernon, P. E. and Parry, J. B. *Personnel Selection in the British Forces.*) What these writers overlook is that it was in those times thought positively desirable to promote adults from the ranks; with educational reform, such a thing is normally no longer necessary.

needs to them in terms that they could understand. The Populists believe that, until native leadership emerges, their vocation is to act as trustees for the technicians. Until last year we thought such belief a pathetic whimsicality. . . .

CHAPTER SEVEN

RICH AND POOR

I. MERIT MONEY

CASTES or classes are universal, and the measure of harmony that prevails within a society is everywhere dependent upon the degree to which stratification is sanctioned by its code of morality. In the long period between the break-up of the old aristocracy and the arrival of the new, there was no agreed standard by which the division into classes could be justified. Conflict about the distribution of privileges and rewards was therefore both harsh and perpetual; and on no topic did feeling run stronger than money. The poor were for ever complaining that the rich had too much for their needs, and demanding more for themselves. The rich were for ever denying the charge, and claiming that, as judged by the contribution they made to the commonwealth, their rewards were too meagre. Between the opposing sides in this arena there could be no peace, at best a compromise truce. What a change there has been! The distribution of rewards has become far more unequal and yet with less strife than before. How has such a happy state arisen? The story must be divided into phases, before and after 2005.

Throughout the last century, as organizations grew bigger and more complex, the spread of incomes necessarily became wider. The industrial ladder lengthened and the number of salary-grades increased. A hundred years ago the small firm with ten employees divided into a mere three or four grades was still quite common.

The top man did not have to be much better off than the bottom. In the larger businesses which came to predominate there had to be hundreds of grades, all differentiated from each other in salary. At the bottom was the man who got no more than the Minimum established as the decent level below which no one should be allowed to fall. Here at any rate there was equality. The Minimum was the foundation from which the whole edifice of incomes rose. In the European Atomic Authority in 1992, for instance, a lift-man received the Minimum of £450 per annum. Above him were the other 221 grades, and as the average differential between the grades was £250, the President of the Authority necessarily had to have an annual income of at least £55,700. His net salary was in fact £60,000 (excluding the Presidential Superannuation Provision). The difference between top and bottom was of the same order of magnitude in most other large organizations, and the smaller firms also had to pay comparable rates in order to attract their share of ability.

It took many years to evolve this order out of the chaos which existed before. The difficult task was to fit the whole array and variety of jobs into an interrelated series of hierarchies, and this was only accomplished when merit rating was developed, to cite an early formula of the British Institute of Management, as 'the systematic assessment of an employee in terms of the performance, aptitudes, and other qualities necessary for the successful carrying out of his job'.[1] There were still arguments when a new kind of job, the product of technical progress, had to be slotted into an existing hierarchy without causing too much disturbance. There were still arguments about the differentials between

1. *Merit rating.* British Institute of Management. 1954.

different levels, and in these the unions might still join if the industrial psychologists could not settle the issue out of hand. But there were no longer serious disputes once merit rating was widely understood and recognized as the proper means of comparing one job with another.

As I have said before, the general mood of our country was never egalitarian. Nearly everyone thought that some people were better than others – either the professional classes were superior to the manual workers or the manual workers were superior to the professional classes – the pity was only that everyone had a different standard by which to judge. In a way it was a relief when more and more people found they could agree about merit, or rather about the meaning which in practice they should give to it, both in education and in industry.

The heat was removed from the old dispute, and a more empirical spirit allowed to play on the scene, as the result of abolishing inherited income. Although they got muddled between the two types, the main body of socialists were far more critical of the inequality due to unearned than to earned income – their stereotype was of the rich man who had inherited a fortune from his father. When death duties, capital levies, capital gains tax, and special super-tax on unearned incomes had done their work, the root of this criticism was cut away, and it was found that very few members of the lower classes had any objection to inequality as such. If a man won a good job after having fought his way up the educational ladder and received a large salary for doing it, why then he probably deserved it – good luck to him.

2. THE MODERN SYNTHESIS

Though this was the general view it was never univer-
sally accepted. Criticism came from the usual quarter.
The egalitarians could not object indefinitely to the
most intelligent children getting the most intensive education. When that happened everyone gained; the
poorest technician was glad if when his wife was ill he
could call a doctor with an I.Q. of at least 100. The
socialists could not indefinitely object to the best people
having the most power. Everyone gained from having
the best men as Chiefs of Staff, Astronomers Royal,
Vice-Chancellors of Universities, or Chairmen of the
Social Science Research Council. The socialists had to
put up with the élite. What a minority of them moaned
about was that it should be so well paid. Granted (some
of them would say), granted that the best astronomer
should be made Royal, why should he get a larger emolu-
ment than the bricklayer who built his observatory?

This was ever an irritating question, since it was in
these terms unanswerable. These strange people rushed
frantically around (and in England of all countries) asking, in an almost metaphysical way, Is this right? Is
that right? The question could of course only be an-
swered by another question, 'Right according to what
principle?' One could say it was wrong to pay one man
more than another because there should be distribution
according to deeds. One could say it was wrong to pay
the lazy scientist more than the diligent dustman because there should be distribution according to effort.
One could say it was wrong to pay the intelligent more
than the stupid because society should compensate for
genetic injustice. One could say it was wrong to pay the
stupid more than the intelligent because society should

compensate for the unhappiness which is the usual lot of the intelligent. (No one can do much about the brilliant, they will be miserable anyway.) One could say it was wrong to pay the man who lived a long and serene life in Upper Slaughter as much as a scientist who wore himself out in the service of knowledge at the Battersea Poly. One could say it was wrong to pay people who liked their work as much as those who didn't. One could – and did – say anything, and whatever one said it was always with the support of the particular kind of justice invoked by principles implicit in the statement.

YES!

To have prised agreement from this arid debate, and to have silenced the socialists for so many years, has been one of the triumphs of modern statecraft. The beauty of it all, for a country which thrives on precedent, is that there has been no sharp break with the past. Tax-free expenses had been becoming a more and more important part of remuneration right through the last century, and by the 1990s a thousand new conventions had struck root. Any knowledgeable historian does not have to do any more than scan the advertisement columns of the newspapers. Here is a fairly typical one of those days:

COUNTY BOROUGH OF HARWELL. *Applications invited for established pensionable post of* ENDOCRINO-PSYCHIATRIST (*Grade 24*) *in Infants Clinic. Salary starting at £10,850 and rising by annual increments of £135 10s to £12,205, with lunches provided. Application forms from Town Psychologist.*

The key words were well understood in local government service. 'Lunches provided' meant that the Borough had, like most other progressive local authorities, subscribed to the convention of the Association of

Municipal Corporations, whereby supplementary payments in kind, from lunches to holidays, were made to graduate staff of the Council.

But why only lunches and holidays and the other fringe benefits? The question was indeed a pertinent one. Was it not the employers' responsibility to ensure that all their staff had a total environment conducive to high performance? After they had been trained at great expense to the public, it was ridiculous to tolerate obstructions, either at home or at work, to their maximum efficiency. For professional staff the division between work and leisure is, after all, purely artificial. Their entire lives are geared to their vocation.

The issue was put squarely over thirty years ago by Mr Gulliver in his plea, famous perhaps just because it was so forthright, for a fair deal for the upper classes. *The Élite's Work is Never Done* – we all remember the title.

We are the thinkers, he said, *are we not? We are paid to think. Well, what do we need to do our work well? We need quiet – no man who is disturbed by noise can devote himself to single-minded concentration. We need comfort – no man who is forced to consider little physical irritations can scale the heights of achievement. We need ample holidays – history shows that scientists have often hit upon the missing link in a chain of thought quite unexpectedly when they were bathing in the sea, walking in the mountains, or drowsing by the Caribbean. A brilliant man can do a full year's work in eight months but not in twelve. We need secretaries at work and domestic servants at home – the chores of life exact energy from the talented which should be devoted to higher things. Just as a carpenter needs a chisel or a mechanic a spanner, we must have books to enlighten, pictures to stimulate, wine to soothe. It is not for ourselves we ask. It is for the good of society, to whose service our brains are dedicated. No jealousy, no vanity, no selfishness must stand in the way of human achievement and social progress.*

The measure of the change is the extent to which these crude ideas have, in a more refined form, secured general acceptance.

Public-spirited employers increasingly adopted the new conception of the duty they owed their staff. Their duty was to provide the best possible conditions for mental activity, during the whole of every twenty-four hours, on the job and off the job. To do this took money, for the purchase of houses, for chauffeurs, for company cars and planes, for domestic service both at a man's work-station and at his home-station, and for wintering at Montego Bay, Tashkent, Kashmir, Caracas, Palm Beach, Llandrindod Wells, or wherever the industrial psychologist recommended. But the money was not in the possession of the employee. He could not do with it just as he pleased. It was not an income but a cost, and as such was rightly borne by the employer.

Mr Idris Roberts was the first politician to see the possibilities in this situation. He could finally spike the critics by agreeing to their demands and establishing complete equality of all incomes. Members of the élite had always opposed equalization on grounds of efficiency: unless, they said, they had adequate incentives they could not be expected to give of their best. But they could readily appreciate that even large incomes, subject to heavy taxation as they were, no longer supplied an incentive to continuous effort. The élite was ready to accept equality because they no longer cared about income, and ordinary people because they still did care about it. Mr Roberts' Equalization of Income Act of

2005 married the interests of all classes in society in a most singular way. Since that time every employee of whatever rank has received the Equal (as emoluments are officially called) simply by virtue of being a citizen, and the differences between grades have been recognized not any longer by salaries but by the payment of such varying expenses as could be justified by the needs of efficiency. Employers have, of course, been allowed to give benefits to technicians too, if they wished, and some of the most enlightened have done so by building cinder-tracks for athletes, concrete pitches for cricketers, and fields for footballers in the grounds of their factories. Technicians have a mere seven-hour stint and so naturally cannot claim the same consideration as professional staff who are in effect on the job for twenty-four hours every day. But morale, although an imponderable, is worth cultivating, and from this point of view wisely administered expenditure out of company funds on such physical amenities is often worth while.

Equalization of income has brought to an end much of the old, wearisome argument about differentials. The only differences now are not between people but between years. Mr Roberts and his reform government recognized that technicians had been accustomed to rises in their incomes from time to time, and if their legitimate expectations had been disappointed, they would have been too. An early sociologist, a Professor Hobhouse, once stated a profound truth.

Question: *What is the ideal income?*
Answer: *Ten per cent more than you've got.*

The Act provided that the Equal drawn out of the common pool by each contributor to it should be adjusted at an annual Price Review. If prices rose in any year, the Equal had to be raised in proportion, and since prices have in fact been increasing steadily since 2005, the ordinary man's remuneration has grown as well. There has been little dispute about the rightness of this procedure, only about the extent to which prices have in fact risen in any twelvemonth. Statisticians from the unions have been known on more than one occasion to produce price indices at the Review quite different from the official ones! What should be treated as an empirical question has been heated up into a political issue. The universities are attending to this. Professors of econometrics are shortly to introduce a more unified curriculum.

The approach to sharing out improvements in efficiency has also been modernized. In the old days technicians used to claim that their 'wages' should go up with productivity. Since, they said, they had produced more, so should they benefit. This was obviously wrong: economic progress is due not to manual workers – they do not even work harder – but to the inventors and organizers who devise new techniques. If anyone is entitled to the increment, it is the meritocracy. Anyway, increases in productivity must be spent on increasing productivity still further and not frittered away on ordinary people. A great country needs great investment. In the middle of last century investment was still pitiably low in Britain, far more so than in Russia, where economic power was securely in the control of an élite who knew that to make their country rich the citizens had to be kept poor. We at last learnt the lesson that productivity and poverty are inseparable. Since 2005 the annual productivity increment has been ploughed back, primarily in human resources, that is, spent upon higher education and upon the maintenance at concert pitch of the people who are its products; and secondarily, upon mechanical equipment of all kinds.

How, one might ask, could anyone object to such a sound, businesslike approach? But they did. The Populists have again managed the seemingly impossible. Let the technicians have a share, they say. Surely the nation can afford it? Productivity has been so buoyant that in 2031 national expenditure − they have even tried to revive the outmoded term, national income − rose by fifty-four per cent, and last year by sixty-one per cent. But these figures are neither here nor there. The agitators speak as if that old socialist myth, the Age of Plenty, had arrived at last. Nothing could be further from the truth. The country needs every scrap of human and material capital it can save if it is to contend with other great nations in the battle for survival. We are all poor, and shall always remain so, because the demands of a scientific age are insatiable. The extremists are, by their loose talk, threatening progress itself.

3. SUMMARY

The reform of the money structure has been one of the most successful of modern times. The perennial disagreements of old sprang from the inevitable conflict between classes when each contained a cross-section of ability. The basic injustice was that intelligent members of the lower classes were not given their due, and in their attack on social disorder, which had for the time being to be waged without forfeiting the support of their classmates of all grades of intelligence, they seized on any and every available principle to justify their protest. When the basic injustice was remedied, and the intelligent from every class were given their full opportunities, those who would have been enemies of the established order became its strongest defenders. Agreement replaced disagreement, and merit was recognized as the principle which should guide economic, as well as educational, reform. But the élite has shown its wisdom, that is, its moderation, by not pushing the principle too far. All citizens even of the lowest class enjoy the same Equal as anyone else, and it is subject to adjustment from year to year.

But even this good order has not escaped criticism. The Populists claim that the appearance of justice is deceptive. They say that the real reason why the 'hypocrisy', as they call us, have got away with so much is that the humble no longer have anyone – except themselves – to speak for them. That the unions are on the side of the establishment because the leaders do not have the capacity to see through, and show up, the double-dealing of the rich who are richer than ever now they are treated as business assets. That the bargaining over the distribution of national expenditure is a battle of wits, and that defeat was bound to go to those who lost their clever children to the enemy. They have therefore ridden into the lists as the self-appointed champions of the lower classes to fight for them in the way the unions can allegedly no longer do. We must admit that their ludicrous demand for a general share-out of increments in productivity has found at least some attentive hearers.

CHAPTER EIGHT

CRISIS

1. THE FIRST WOMEN'S CAMPAIGN

I HAVE been trying to describe the growth of our society, particularly since 1944, in such a way as to reveal some of the deep-rooted causes of our present discontents. I do not gainsay the achievements of social engineering. I do not deny the fact of progress. I do maintain, however, that society never works smoothly. Despite all the advances of the last century, sociology is still in its infancy, and until it has reached the eminence of its fellow sciences, we shall not know with any certainty the muster of laws which social engineering must obey. The Nature of human beings is still the most mysterious of all. As it is, the society we have contrived is no more than a counterpoise of opposing forces held in always delicate equilibrium. Every change creates its counter. The opening of schools to talent was bound to anger some of the old cast down from their seats. Demotion for the stupid children of upper-class origin was bound to grieve their parents, and so forth – all the reactions I have mentioned before. My submission is that these at present inescapable strains account in some measure for the support upon which the extremists have been able to draw. I readily agree, however, that while this historical analysis may go some way to explain the possibility of such a movement, it does not explain why the movement has cohered in this particular form. What is the immediate pattern of organization? And what the spark?

The first and most obvious point to make is that the most prominent present leaders of the Populists are all women, and have been so since the first decade of the century. That was the time when women first began to come to the fore in left-wing politics, and, as one would expect, their first essay was in the romantic style that suits them best. Taking their cue from the Russian Populists[1] of the previous century after whom the modern movement is named, shaggy young girls from Newnham and Somerville, instead of taking the jobs as surgeons and scientists for which their education fitted them, scattered to Salford and Newcastle to become factory workers, ticket collectors, and air hostesses. They used lipstick, watched football matches, and went to Butlins for their holidays. They believed it was their mission to live as common technicians and by so doing to rouse them to a sense of the indignities from which they should feel they suffered. They joined the technical unions, stood for office, and agitated for strike action. They chained themselves to the seats of the British Productivity Council. They petitioned the T.U.C. to commit itself to 'Socialism'. They sent propaganda far and wide. Perhaps their strangest achievement was the capture of *The Times* and its conversion, for a few months in 2009, into a popular newspaper. Even so, all their efforts were in vain. For the spark there was no tinder. The girls went home to Tunbridge

1. These were composed of young intellectuals who on return from universities abroad decided, under the influence of Bakunin, Kropotkin, and Stepniak, to go to the people for inspiration, dressed themselves as peasants, lived in the villages, and tried to promote revolution. When the peasants merely gaped at them, they were driven to terrorism. Fortunately there were no Sophie Perovskayas in England; it is not easy to imagine British women with a bomb, hydrogen or any other kind.

Wells and Bath, and the great majority of the technicians continued to go calmly about their daily occasions, sharing in the general stability of employment, intent on the interests of their children. They were tolerantly amused by these antics; they were not moved to action. There is ordinarily no one so stolid as ordinary British technicians. They are the salt of the earth.

But before they all went home, the girls struck up a strange alliance which has left a permanent mark on our subsequent political affairs. In the inner councils of the Technicians Party there were still some aged men who after having received their early training in the ancient Labour Party had never emerged from their political adolescence. The old men were attracted to the young girls, and perhaps now and then it happened the other way round as well. They began to draft programmes and policies. Why, they asked, did the girls fail? They failed, went the answer, because they were not really technicians themselves. Their minds worked differently. They thought in the idiom of Somerville, not Salford. They had no feeling for the technicians' real problems. And therefore they were distrusted. But what if these girls, and even boys, with high I.Q.s, never left the technical classes? What if they refused to go to the universities? What if they left school at the same time as ordinary people? Then they would be trusted. They would be technicians at heart, if élite in brain. Their high intelligence at the service of their fellows, they would give the leadership that men like Bevin and Citrine once gave to the old trade unions. A new socialist movement would be built up from the grass roots, new meaning given to the old slogans of equality. It was a dazzling prospect.

But when it came to practical proposals all the planners could suggest was that a proportion of the more able children in each generation should leave school at the minimum age and become technicians themselves. But how would they be chosen? By ballot? Some of them played with this idea, even suggesting that every tenth person among the over 125s, a tithe of the intelligence in every generation, should be allocated to technical work. This was obvious nonsense, and was never pressed. But if not by ballot, then how? The reformers ended by proposing that teachers should stop bringing pressure on parents and children who were not keen on higher education. They wanted the Parent-Teachers Associations abolished, so that parents would be less influenced by the teachers. They actually wanted schools to close the evening and week-end classes for parents. They wanted all sorts of things that were clearly no longer practicable. The plain fact was (and is) that most clever people want to get on in the world. There was little need for the schools to encourage. The children agreed with teacher before she spoke.

In their dilemma the dissidents then turned back to an old idea much in vogue in the century before 1944 – the idea that manual work was as valuable as mental. For a long time indeed, though never in any Communist country, the adherents of Karl Marx's labour theory of value professed to believe that manual work was actually *more* valuable than any other sort. (A strange idea, it seems to us, yet the historian can have no doubt it was once widely accepted.) And the theorists went on to urge a revival of these old notions. They really had no alternative. They had to admit that most clever children wanted to become brain-workers. They also thought the children wrong. Since they wanted the children to become manual workers of their own voluntary choice, they had to argue that the children *should* be satisfied to do manual work. In other words the very system of values had to change! They could reach no other conclusion. They said that the carpenter was as important as the crystallographer, ignoring the awkward fact that none of the theorists was a carpenter.

The agitators of twenty-five years ago were led on to ask more and more questions about society. From these discussions derive the modern theories of equality with which we are grappling today. Why, they asked, is one man regarded as superior to another? It is, they said, because we put up with such narrowness in the paramount values, or criteria, by which men judge one another's worth. When Britain was governed by warriors who depended for their power on their ability to kill, the great fighter was the great man; and thinkers, poets, and painters were treated with scorn. When Britain was governed by landowners, men who made their living by trade or preaching or singing were all lesser breeds. When Britain was governed by manufacturers, all other men were regarded as inferior. But, they say, there has never been such gross over-simplification as in modern Britain. Since the country is dedicated to the one overriding purpose of economic expansion, people are judged according to the single test of how much they increase production, or the knowledge that will, directly or indirectly, lead to that consummation. If they do as little as the ordinary manual worker, they are of no account. If they do as much as the scientist whose invention does the work of ten thousand, or the administrator who organizes whole clutches of technicians, then they are among the great.

The ability to raise production, directly or indirectly, is known as 'intelligence': this iron measure is the judgement of society upon its members.[1] 'Intelligence' is as much qualification for power in the modern state as 'breeding' was in the old. The stress on this sort of ability was produced by a century of wars and threats of war, in which the kind of occupational achievement which raised the national war-potential was lauded above all else; but, say the theorists, now that the threat is no longer so immediate, can we not encourage a diversity of values?

In 2009 a local group of the Technicians Party issued the 'Chelsea Manifesto'. Although it attracted little public attention at the time, it has had a considerable influence, especially within the movement, during the last decade. It is a long and turgid document which begins by claiming (in an interpretation which no historian could accept) that the primary aim of the group, as of all their socialist predecessors and of the Church before them, is to cultivate variety. Their goal is the classless society. They oppose inequality because it reflects a narrowness of values. They deny that one man is in any fundamental way the superior of another. They seek the equality of man in the sense that they want every man to be respected for the good that is in him. Every man is a genius at something, even every woman, they say: it is the function of society to discover and honour it, whether it is genius at making pots, growing daisies, ringing bells, caring for babies, or even (to show their tolerance) genius at inventing radio telescopes. It

1. They have, of course, no use for the orthodox view that it is the very complication of modern society which demands the sort of basic intelligence which can speedily relate one part of a complex whole to another.

is perhaps worth quoting the last paragraph of the Manifesto; this summarizes the writers' odd views on what a classless society would be like.

The classless society would be one which both possessed and acted upon plural values. Were we to evaluate people, not only according to their intelligence and their education, their occupation, and their power, but according to their kindliness and their courage, their imagination and sensitivity, their sympathy and generosity, there could be no classes. Who would be able to say that the scientist was superior to the porter with admirable qualities as a father, the civil servant with unusual skill at gaining prizes superior to the lorry-driver with unusual skill at growing roses? The classless society would also be the tolerant society, in which individual differences were actively encouraged as well as passively tolerated, in which full meaning was at last given to the dignity of man. Every human being would then have equal opportunity, not to rise up in the world in the light of any mathematical measure, but to develop his own special capacities for leading a rich life.

The Manifesto reveals its archaism most quaintly in the supporter whom it rustles forth from his grave – not one of the modern scientific 'divines' but, of all people, the almost-forgotten Matthew Arnold. It actually italicizes the absurd notion of 'culture' in his *Culture and Anarchy* – which 'does not try to teach down to the level of inferior classes; it does not try to win them for this or that sect of its own, with ready-made judgements and watchwords. It seems to do away with classes; to make the best that has been thought and known in the world current everywhere; to make all men live in an atmosphere of sweetness and light, where they may use ideas, as it uses them itself, freely – nourished and not bound by them.' Oh God, oh Galton!

In the light of this approach the authors of the Manifesto sought to give a new meaning to equality of opportunity. This, they said, should not mean equal opportunity to rise up in the social scale, but equal opportunity for all people, irrespective of their 'intelligence', to develop the virtues and talents with which they are endowed, all their capacities for appreciating the beauty and depth of human experience, all their potential for living to the full. The child, every child, is a precious individual, not just a potential functionary of society. The schools should not be tied to the occupational structure, bent on turning out people for the jobs at any particular moment considered important, but should be devoted to encouraging all human talents, whether or not these are of the kind needed in a scientific world. The arts and manual skills should be given as much prominence as science and technology. The Manifesto urged that the hierarchy of schools should be abolished and common schools at last established. These schools should have enough good teachers so that all children should have individual care and stimulus. They could then develop at their own pace to their own particular fulfilment. The schools would not segregate the like but mingle the unlike; by promoting diversity within unity, they would teach respect for the infinite human differences which are not the least of mankind's virtues. The schools would not regard children as shaped once and for all by Nature, but as a combination of potentials which can be cultivated by Nurture.

2. MODERN FEMINIST MOVEMENT

These first phases of reformism are important to us today because they saw the formulation of the ideas which have since become so notorious. In point of organization there has been little continuity. That generation of malcontents returned home and many of them are now the respected wives of some of our leading scientists. But not all; some did not marry, some kept their rebellious spirit alive in the nursery. They have been joined by further recruits from some of the best homes in the country, culminating in the rush of the last three years. Why so many women[1] up in arms? It is not altogether easy to explain. I would, however, be no aspirant to sociology were I to allow any role to accident. That would, I believe, be a serious misinterpretation. It is worth noting, what is sometimes forgotten, that there were several excellent studies made of female psychology towards the end of last century before the resurgence in politics. The gist of them was that society seemed to many women, especially the able ones, in mind men if at heart women, to have been constructed expressly for the convenience of the opposite sex. Are there not, the indignant asked, as many intelligent girls born every year as there are boys? They get much the same education as any male cadet for the meritocracy. But what happens then? They take the post for which they have been trained only until they marry. From that moment they are expected, for a few years at any rate, to devote themselves to their children. The sheer drudgery of their lives has been much relieved by the revival of domestic service and the help of husbands. But they cannot, if they take any notice of the teaching

1. Dr Puffin (of York University in an unpublished M.Sc. thesis) has pointed out how difficult it is to get reliable figures for membership, and asserts that, on a count he made at the Populist Convention at Leicester, women only numbered sixty-two per cent of the delegates, the rest being men, with the old predominating.

of psychology, entrust the entire care of their offspring to a person of low intelligence. Infants need the love of a mother; they also need her intellectual stimulation, her tender introduction to a high culture, her diligent preparation for a dedicated life. She will neglect her motherly duties only at the peril of her children, not to speak of the displeasure of her husband.

What these early studies showed were that this dual role – in her chosen profession and in her biological vocation – often gave rise to mental tension in all those women who could not feel that child-rearing is (as it is in fact) one of the noblest occupations of them all, especially when it is part-time. The problem has never been an easy one to solve. Some women have taken their own way out by limiting the size of their families so that they can return to paid work as soon as possible – with the unfortunate result that the stock of intelligence has been endangered. Others have denounced the traditional family as an anachronism and transferred their motherly role entirely to servants. Others have signed the pledge that they would send their children only to the London School of Arts and Crafts, where science is not taught at all! Yet others, a small but significant minority, have been lured by the old mystique of equality. The early striving for social equality was greatly strengthened by its association with the movement for emancipation of women. Equality irrespective of sex or class – it was a good slogan, only it lost much of its appeal when hereditary classes, though not hereditary sexes, were gradually abolished. But for some women the appeal remained as bright as ever. As they saw it, the sexes were treated as 'unequal'. They wanted sex equality, but since this is obviously unobtainable, they displaced their antagonism from men in general on to the 'ruling classes', the scapegoat whom they imagined to be in some way responsible for the dictatorship of biology. It was all the easier to vent their antagonism because many of them had time on their hands, once their children entered nursery school, which they could devote to discussions in their women's circles. Most of them did not react by going to the extreme of refusing to make use of domestic service. The determination of so many of the present leaders of the movement to do all their own household work is unusual and in some ways welcome since it means the married ones have little time left over for political organization.

Through the women's circles, the activists have been able to assert their influence and show their menfolk, who perhaps show too little humility about the wonders with which they have furnished our estate, that they are a force to be reckoned with. In so doing they are making a protest against the standards, those of achievement, by which men assess each other. Women have always been judged more by what they *are* than by what they *do*, more for other personal qualities than for their intelligence; more for their warmth of heart, their vivacity, and their charm than for their worldly success. It is therefore understandable that they should wish to stress their own virtues, only regrettable that in this the quality have joined with women of no more than ordinary ability.

Astringency has been added to the debate, first, by the 'impoverishment' of women, and second, by the eugenic campaign. The impoverishment is the result of the reform of remuneration which I described in the last chapter. Men are paid as business assets, and housewives cannot ordinarily pretend to be only that. Élite wives benefit indirectly from the new conception of home as just a branch office. Their servants are on the employer's expenditure roll. But they do not benefit as much as men. They do not attend so many stylish business dinners at the employer's expense; they do not need to travel abroad so often; they do not have two bars, one at work as well as one at home. Naturally they sometimes resent the privileged standard of living which their husbands, as business assets, have to enjoy whether they like it or not. This is one reason why the sex war has embraced politics.

Then there has been the eugenic campaign. This was founded on ordinary common sense. Professor Eagle and his collaborators were really saying, to begin with, that before choosing their marriage partners people should consult the intelligence register. This was obviously in the national interest; it was also in the interest of happy marriage. No man with a high I.Q. could in the long run be as proud of a child destined for a secondary modern school as of one destined for Oxford; yet the chance of such an unhappy issue was obviously greater, the lower the intelligence of the woman he married. A high-I.Q. man who mates with a low-I.Q. woman is simply wasting his genes and it is therefore common prudence for him to examine the records of her father and grandfather as well. Hence the success story of the pretty young mother who discovers she is going to be all right after all, the Registry has wrongly docketed her grandfather – it has become a favourite theme of popular fiction. Altogether this was, one would think, sensible advice. At any rate many men but not all – for what age is not an age of lust? – have thought so. It is now rare for a sober senior civil servant to consider marriage with any girl who cannot produce an I.Q. of over 130 at some point in her intelligence genealogy. For one thing, if he married beneath him there would be too great a danger of the news spreading through his department, and nothing would more surely give him the reputation of unreliability.

But women – and for once I am bound to confess I do not understand why – have not taken so kindly to this advice. Where, they ask, is the romance in an intelligenic marriage? And to underline their question they have echoed the lower classes who esteem bodily prowess and give a heightened value, a sort of symbolic value, to a superficial quality not at all related to intelligence, that is, to appearance. Beauty has become their flag. The more energetically Professor Eagle campaigns against men who choose women for their appearance – he has been most ably assisted by his wife – the more do the Populists decry his efforts, and the more often do the chic cadres attend their own meetings clad in the most extravagant clothes, with Salpanas on their shoulders, and sandals on their feet, their faces decorated in the most beguiling way and their hair styled according to the latest decrees from the fashion committee. One of their favourite slogans is the ridiculous 'Beauty is achievable by all'. The remarkable appearance of the women members of the 'flying seminar' cannot be denied. They are not the sort of people who wear wool next to their skin.

3. COMING OF THE CRISIS

Without the events to which I will now turn, this women's movement would have been no more than a high-spirited charade. It has been rendered a threat to the State by the sudden crystallization of an issue which has long remained submerged. I refer, of course, to the enunciation of the new revolutionary doctrine on the right wing of the Conservative Party. Lord Cecil and his followers have done what no one has dared to do within living memory: they have actually urged – not in so many words but that is their regrettable tenor – that the hereditary principle should be openly restored to its former pride of place. The shock has been profound. Extremism on the right has always led to extremism on the left.

Their plea cannot be ignored, for they claim that they are only seeking the stamp of public approval for a trend which has been evident for at least twenty-five years. The fact is that every advance towards equality of opportunity creates resistance to going any further. A century ago educational reform was vital to reduce the waste of ability in the lower classes. But every time intelligence was skimmed off and transferred to the upper classes, the reasons for continuing the process were correspondingly weakened. By 1990 or thereabouts all adults with I.Q.s of more than 125 belonged to the meritocracy. A high proportion of the children with I.Q.s over 125 were the children of these same adults. The top of today are breeding the top of tomorrow to a greater extent than at any time in the past. The élite is on the way to becoming hereditary; the principles of heredity and merit are coming together. The vital transformation which has taken more than two centuries to accomplish is almost complete.

The meritocracy is undoubtedly more brilliant as a result. Fifty years ago many members of the élite were first-generation, and for that very reason suffered in comparison with their fellows. They came from homes in which there was no tradition of culture.[1] Their parents, without a good education themselves, were not able to augment the influence exercised by the teacher. These clever people were in a sense only half-educated, in school but not home. When they graduated they had not the same self-assurance as those who had the support and stimulus of their families from the beginning. They were often driven by this lack of self-confidence to compulsive conformity, thus weakening the power of innovation which it is one of the chief functions of the élite to wield. They were often intolerant, even more competitive in their striving for ascent than was necessary, and yet too cautious to succeed. Now that so many of the élite are second-generation or better, these faults are no longer so evident, and society is no longer courting the risk of degenerating into a stratified mob. No longer is it so necessary to debase standards by attempting to extend a higher civilization to the children of the lower classes. This is what the new Conservatives allege. They claim that the advantages of the new disposition should be frankly recognized – even to the extent of allowing to the élite not only the privileges which are their accepted right but also, and this is the moot point, the guarantee of a privileged education for their children.

The shock administered by this demand has in a way

1. One of the signs of the times is that T. S. Eliot is much read again – that is, his *Notes towards the Definition of Culture*. Particularly his words 'An élite, if it is a governing élite, so far as the natural impulse to pass on to one's offspring both power and prestige is not artificially checked, will tend to establish itself as a class.' Less often quoted are the words that follow 'But an élite which thus transforms itself tends to lose its function as an élite, for the qualities by which the original members won their position will not all be transmitted equally to their descendants.'

been aggravated by some of the recent advances in the social sciences, whose consequences seem, quite independently, to threaten some of our most cherished beliefs. The fact is that the accumulation of knowledge in psychology has made it possible to identify the intelligence and aptitudes of the individual at ever earlier ages. Up to the turn of the century, there was still such a margin of error about the tests as they were applied, even at fourteen, that if people had had their last chance at that age much ability would have been lost to the nation. The late developers could not be neglected if full meaning was to be given to equality of opportunity. Hence modern adult education. Hence the regional centres. Hence the opportunity for anyone to have himself re-tested at any stage of life. But step by step the rapid advances in their discipline have given the educational psychologists the means to identify intelligence during childhood, even though it is so far latent that the untrained observer cannot detect it, and to forecast the age in adult life at which it *will* develop. These discoveries weakened the rationale of the adult education movement. If on the basis of tests at the age of fifteen, the experts could predict the future, what purpose was any longer served by the Regional Centres? The experts merely had to tag the late developer and, at the appropriate age, confirm that their prediction was correct. Provided they made generous allowance for border-line cases, they could not go wrong. The organizers of adult education have fought against this iconoclasm (as it seems to them) and, quite apart from disputing the validity of the new findings, have argued that their movement should continue if only to maintain the morale of low-I.Q. subjects who would otherwise be without hope.

The test-ages at which highly reliable predictions could be made have become steadily lower. In 2000, the reliable age was nine; in 2015, the reliable age was four; in 2020 it was three. This was as severe a blow to many teachers as the earlier discoveries had been to the adult educators. The real justification for a common education in primary schools for everyone up to eleven was that no one could be quite sure of the ultimate value of any young boy or girl. It was only fair that they should not be segregated until their I.Q.s were finally known. But when ability could once be tested and identified at the age of three, there was really no point at all in the brighter children going to the same co-intellectual school as others who would almost inevitably retard their development. It was much more sensible to segregate outstanding children from the ruck in separate kindergartens and primary schools, just in the same way as at the top the outstanding young people sent to Oxford and Cambridge were divided off from the others who could not rank any higher than the provincial universities. The late developers could remain with the *hoi polloi* until their time came, or be sent to experimental schools where the processes of nature would be hurried forward.

Faced with these facts, some teachers reacted in the same way as the adult educators and said, granted that the R.A. is three, it is still necessary to pretend that it is not. Children cannot be condemned so early: they will cease to strive when they know that no effort will prove the psychologist wrong, except within a small margin of error. They must be given the stimulus of hope; so must the teachers, and so also, above all, must their parents. Any sociologist must admit the strength of the argument. Equality of opportunity has for so long been the ethos of education that it will not do to abandon it overnight. So important is social cohesion that we shall have to make haste slowly.

But science does not move slowly. Three was not the limit. The R.A. was in effect pushed back into the womb. Dr Charles, the Nobel Prizewinner who has taught us so much about the mode of transmission of intellectual ability, has recently shown that the intelligence of children could at last be safely predicted from the intelligence of their forbears. His early and remarkable experiments on progeny testing were with rats. His X-hypothesis was later confirmed by the wide-scale census tests of all three-year-old babies in 2016. In Britain, at any rate, Eugenics House already has records for four generations, from the 1950s onwards, as well as a large number of retrospective estimates compiled as the result of the most painstaking research, particularly since the study of obituaries became a recognized branch of sociology. By using these records, and making all necessary allowances, the ability of the offspring of any couple can be forecast with remarkable accuracy; and indeed, on various assumptions about marriage habits, and inward and outward migration, intelligence trends and distributions have actually been calculated for the next 1,000 years.

4. NEW CONSERVATISM

Dr Charles's work has undoubtedly helped to alter the attitudes of intelligent parents. They no longer need to send their children to an ordinary primary school, and if the State will not provide special ones, they are already in a few districts establishing private schools, where their children will mix only with their own special class.

They no longer need to look questioningly into their cots, not knowing what kind of education the occupants will eventually deserve. Their children are, in their eyes, not just children but rulers born to a high destiny. All this has led to hardening of class sentiment. Once the need for common treatment of all children up to a minimum age was questioned, once the foundations of society were shaken in this way, some intelligent parents were stimulated to go further and ask whether equality of opportunity is not a wholly outdated idea.

If the argument ended there, we defenders of the existing social order would not rest too uneasy. The flaw in the reasoning thus far is obvious, and all but the most bigoted and family-loving of the Conservatives, who have not even read Charles, heard of Galton, or paid attention to the most elementary genetics, are aware of it. The flaw is that intelligent people tend, on the whole, to have less intelligent children than themselves; the tendency is for there to be a continuous regression[1] towards the mean – stupid people bearing slightly more clever children as surely as clever people have slightly less. If it were not so, a ruling élite, once established, would rightly be hereditary. As it is, this brute fact makes some degree of social mobility essential, even though it need not be as great as a century ago.

As I say, most of the Conservative leaders are fully

1. The phenomenon of regression was well understood even in my special period of history, that just as children of tall parents tended to be tall, though not so tall as their parents, so with intelligence. As Professor Eysenck said, 'The average I.Q. of members of the higher professional and administrative classes is in the neighbourhood of 150; that of their children is slightly in excess of 120. The lower professional and technical executive groups have I.Q.s in the neighbourhood of 130; their children tend to be in the 115 region on the average.' *The Uses and Abuses of Psychology*, 1953.

apprised of the tendency towards regression and have tried to take account of it in their schemes. Their proposals differ, in emphasis if not in kind. The most extreme right-wing asks, what does it matter? A few stupid children of clever parents may receive higher education – and most of them will not be all that less intelligent than their parents; but the polish given them in their homes will fit them to succeed to the élite, which they will man with no disgrace, if not adorn. Any loss of effectiveness in the meritocracy will be more than outweighed by the benefits of making it hereditary. Parents will be easier in their minds and their children will not have to go through all the psychological stresses of having to prove themselves in competition with children from the lower classes. Nor will ambitions have to be aroused in the minds of all parents, however stupid, lest their children escape the attentions of education; and if their ardours can be left cool, the body politic will gain in stability. A further wave of social mobility may be necessary later on, they say, if the distribution of intelligence gets too much out of line with the distribution of power; but let it wait; give us a half-century of peace from the pandemonium of social mobility.

Such professions have no chance of acceptance, they represent too sharp a break with our ethos. A more subtle school urges that the distribution of intelligence should be adjusted to the existing distribution of power; although the approach is the opposite of what the educational system aims at doing, the goal is the same. Some encouragement has been given to this group by the experiments carried out by Academician Donikin at Ulan-Bator, which cap a long sequence in many other countries, including our own. If the reports are to be believed, the biophysicists there have shown how,

n the lower animals at any rate, controlled mutations
n the genetic constitutions of the unborn can be induced by means of radiation so as to raise the level of
intelligence above that which would otherwise be
yielded. Were anything really practical to come of this,
the crucial question would be, whose children are to
have their intelligence artificially raised in this manner? The Conservative leaders claim that those who
already have should have more, as the surrounding
environment which the parents could provide would
then be as favourable as possible to the nurturing of
capacity; and that it would be absurd to tinker with
ordinary have-nots since they already have quite as
much ability as they need for their allotted functions.
Obviously the decision must rest with the meritocracy,
not the democracy who have no means of weighing the
gravity of the issue. I recognize that any increase in
knowledge must be welcomed for its own sake, but all
the same I am bound to say that, speaking from the
standpoint of sociology, the application of such knowledge, rather than its acquisition, cannot proceed too
slowly. The rumours that have circulated about the
tampering with the wives of leading civil servants at the
Volunteer Maternity Centre on South Uist have already
caused much alarm.

Meanwhile, it has been proposed that the Ministry
of Education should at once make its Adoption of Children scheme mandatory upon all local authorities.
Adoption of children is as old as man. Always, in all
societies, would-be parents, unfortunate enough to have
had no children themselves, or not as many as they
would have liked, have sought out the kind of infants
most approved – bonny-looking and chubby, fair with
blue eyes, dark with grey eyes, boys or girls, small or

big. The difference between us and other people in other times and other places is that we value intelligence more, and that the psychologists and biologists have given us the means of estimation even in the cradle. A genius without parents automatically becomes a ward of state. An intelligent orphan is now a prize for any family, especially for wives who are not prepared to seduce leading professors or seek artificial insemination from the few highly intelligent men attested by the Ministry as I.Q.-donors. The normal demand upon the Adoption Societies has been multiplied in recent years by members of the élite who wish to fill their quiver. The supply is grossly deficient; hence the disturbing growth in the black-market baby traffic, stupid babies from élite homes being sent, sometimes with princely dowries,[1] in exchange for clever ones from the lower classes. Desperate parents have even descended to baby-snatching after keeping a watch on pregnant mothers of the lower classes whose intelligence genealogies are promising. Private detectives and geneticists have worked together in a scandalous compact. Better, plead the culprits, to adopt the élite into their future class when they are tiny than to do it much later and in a much more cumbersome way through the 'foster parents' of grammar school and university. After a very full government inquiry the Welfare of Children Act was passed in 2030. It provided that private adoptions should henceforth be void unless the local authority in the area where the adopting parents lived had intro-

1. In *Rook v. Partner* (4 QB, 2028) it was alleged that Mr and Mrs Rook had promised £150,000 in exchange for an I.Q. of 140, and a sum of £50,000 to the doctor who arranged the deal. Mr Justice Finch's animadversions in his summing up led to the setting up of the Salmon Committee on the Adoption of Children.

luced the model scheme, and conformed to the safeguards, laid down by the Ministry of Education. The
Cheltenham, Bournemouth, Harrogate, and Bognor
Education Committees immediately took advantage of
his permissive Act, but their lead has so far been fol-
owed by very few other L.E.A.s. The demand of many
Conservatives is that all local authorities should now be
obliged to comply, and it is this, on top of everything
else, which precipitated the crisis of last May.

5. A RANK AND FILE AT LAST

The sociologist, with his trained insight, can perhaps
understand even more clearly than others why these
events, and the discussions surrounding them, have
caused such a profound revulsion. Any hint, let alone
the assertion in influential quarters, that the hereditary
principle should be restored, after the struggles of two
centuries to destroy it, is tantamount to an attack on the
core and centre of our value system, and one all the
more disquieting because events have moved so swiftly.
Even the upholders of the lower classes, the Owenites,
the Chartists, and the Socialists, were not as shocking
as this to their social superiors two centuries ago. Those
rebels could at least profess their affinity with the
Christian religion. These other rebels, of the right as
they are, cannot claim any such respectable descent:
the doctrine of equal opportunity has won a complete
ascendancy in the realm of practical ethics. The Conservatives want two luxuries at once – the luxury of
inheritance and the luxury of efficiency. But they cannot have them both. They have to choose, and they have
chosen wrongly. Could we tolerate men as Directors of
Eugenics House, of the Centre at South Uist, even as

Prime Ministers, although that admittedly does not matter so much, who enjoyed power merely because they had clever fathers? Could we tolerate the clever sons of stupid fathers wasting their lives in some dingy Union office in Manchester? We could not. The sanction for such folly would be sharp. China and Africa would draw ahead in productivity. British and European influence would fade as our science became clumbered up by the second-rate. We should once again be 'over-matched in the competition of the world'? Does one need to say more? So obvious is it, that the Populists can now parade as protectors of what is best in our established society. A phantasmagoria indeed!

Public opinion surveys have shown that the disturbances have been fired more by a sentiment of opposition to the Conservatives than by a sentiment of loyalty to the Populists. Whatever the combination of motives there is no doubt about what happened. Every little dispute, which would ordinarily have been quietly smoothed out in the course of conciliation, has instead been charged with a bitterness without parallel in modern times. The events at Stevenage, Kirkcaldy, and South Shields, the action of the domestic servants, the deputations sent to the Ministry of Education and the T.U.C. – all overflowed their nominal purpose in a very flood of rebellion. A thousand petty grievances became one.

Many of those who demonstrated were, of course, quite inarticulate about their aims, being reduced to incoherent murmuring when asked, in Court, to express themselves. They looked for upper-class leadership, and found it in the only one bizarre quarter where it existed. The women's circles, and their leaders, Urania O'Connor, Lady Avocet, and the Countess of Perth, did not reate the movement, the movement created them, and the study of social history had not (until the last few ears) been so neglected, it would have been obvious all that such is the custom of politics. The women erely had to seize their historic opportunity, which ey have done to the best of their considerable ability. hey sailed when the wind blew. Bonds have been rmed between the women's circles and dissident techicians of very different levels of intelligence, indeed ith the dissidents from every walk of life whom I ave described in previous chapters. Long moribund ranches of the Technicians Party have been suddenly isited with hundreds of applicants for membership. The ommotion came to a head in the Leicester Convention, here the Populists issued their now celebrated charter.

What a strange document this is! With its echoes om the past in the quotations from the now longrgotten Tawney and Cole, William Morris and John all, the authors dress out their claim to be the 'heirs' this word was surely a mistake?) of one of the great treams in British history. But they dare not vouchsafe ore than a few trite words about domestic service lest heir intelligent ladies desert them. They dare not spouse equality too openly, lest their upper-class suporters take fright, though they came perilously close to t in the section of the peroration which starts 'Oh, isters'. When stripped of its decoration the charter conains few concrete demands apart from the banning of doptions; the preservation of primary schools and adult ducation centres; more allowance for age and experince in industrial promotion; giving the technicians a hare in increasing productivity; and, most revolutionry and perhaps most meaningful, even a trifle nostalic, to a historian, the raising of the school-leaving age

to eighteen, and the creation of 'common secondary
schools for all'. On their face-value these demands do
not constitute a political programme of more than the
crudest sort, but the authors could not go further to
concentrate the loyalties of their very diverse followers without antagonizing some of those upon whose support they lean.

6. FROM HERE, WHERE?

It was not my purpose in this essay to predict the course
of events next May, but rather to show that the movement of protest had deep roots in our history. If my
view be accepted, opposition even to the greatest institutions of modern society is inevitable. The hostility
now manifest has long been latent. For more than half
a century, the lower classes have been harbouring
resentments which they could not make articulate
until the present day.

If I have succeeded in adding at all to understanding
of this complex story and persuaded any of my fellows
not to take present discontents *too* lightly, my purpose
has been well achieved. But I am mindful that I may
be expected to say a word about what is likely to happen. It can, of course, be no more than a personal
opinion on which any reader of these pages is as well
tutored as myself. Nevertheless, I hold firmly to the
belief that May 2034 will be at best an 1848, on the
English model at that. There will be stir enough. The
universities may shake. There will be other disturbances later on as long as the Populists survive. But on
this occasion anything more serious than a few days'
strike and a week's disturbance, which it will be well
within the capacity of the police (with their new
weapons) to quell, I do not for one moment envisage.

The reason I have already referred to. The charter is too vague. The demands are, with one exception, not in any way a fundamental challenge to the government. This is no revolutionary movement but a caucus of disparate groups held together only by a few charismatic personalities and an atmosphere of crisis. There is no tradition of political organization on which to draw. There are, indeed, already signs of dissension within the camp, as the result of the wise concessions which have been made. Since I began to write this essay a fortnight ago, the Chairman of the Social Science Research Council has proffered his weighty recommendations to the government. The Prime Minister quickly acted on these counsels of moderation, instructed Weather Control to bring on autumn a month early and announced, in his speech on 25 September at Kirkcaldy itself, that his party was going to expel half a dozen of its right-wing members, that the adoption scheme would not be made mandatory for the present, that equality of opportunity would be maintained as official policy, and that there was no intention at present of tampering with the primary schools or with adult education. His speech has, as *The Times* put it, 'stolen the girls' thunder'.

Behind the shift and turn of current politics is the underlying fact with which I opened my essay. The last century has witnessed a far-reaching redistribution of ability between the classes in society, and the consequence is that the lower classes no longer have the power to make revolt effective. For a short moment they may prosper through an alliance with the odd and passing disillusion of a section of the upper classes. But such *déclassé* people can never be more than an eccentric minority – the Populists have never been more than that as a serious political force – because the élite is treated with all the wise distinction that any heart can desire. Without intelligence in their heads, the lower classes are never more menacing than a rabble, even if they are sometimes sullen, sometimes mercurial, not yet completely predictable. If the hopes of some earlier dissidents had been realized and the brilliant children from the lower classes remained there, to teach, to inspire, and to organize the masses, then I should have had a different story to tell. The few who now propose such a radical step are a hundred years too late. This is the prediction I shall expect to verify when I stand next May listening to the speeches from the great rostrum at Peterloo.[1]

1. Since the author of this essay was himself killed at Peterloo, the publishers regret they were not able to submit to him the proofs of his manuscript, for the corrections he might have wished to make before publication. The text, even this last section, has been left exactly as he wrote it. The failings of sociology are as illuminating as its successes.